Historical American Biographies

EUGENE V. DEBS

Outspoken Labor Leader and Socialist

Charles W. Carey, Jr.

Enslow Publishers, Inc.

40 Industrial Road	PO Box 38
Box 398	Aldershot
Berkeley Heights, NJ 07922	Hants GU12 6BP
USA	UK

http://www.enslow.com

Library of Congress Cataloging-in-Publication Data

Carey, Charles W.
    Eugene V. Debs : outspoken labor leader and socialist / Charles W.
Carey, Jr.
       p. cm. — (Historical American biographies)
    Summary: A biography of the trade union leader, political activist, and
pacifist who ran five times as the socialist candidate for president.
    Includes bibliographical references and index.
    ISBN 0-7660-1979-9
    1. Debs, Eugene V. (Eugene Victor), 1855-1926—Juvenile literature.
2. Socialists—United States—Biography—Juvenile literature. 3. Labor
leaders—United States—Biography—Juvenile literature. [1. Debs, Eugene
V. (Eugene Victor), 1855-1926. 2. Labor leaders. 3. Socialists.] I. Title.
II. Series.
    HX84.D3 C33   2003
    335'.3'092—dc21

                               2002153082
Printed in the United States of America

10 9 8 7 6 5 4 3 2 1

To Our Readers:
We have done our best to make sure all Internet Addresses in this book were
active and appropriate when we went to press. However, the author and the pub-
lisher have no control over and assume no liability for the material available on
those Internet sites or on other Web sites they may link to. Any comments or sug-
gestions can be sent by e-mail to comments@enslow.com or to the address on the
back cover.

Illustration Credits: Courtesy of Indiana State University, pp. 18, 109,
112; Enslow Publishers, Inc., p. 16; Photo courtesy Eugene V. Debs
Foundation, Terre Haute, Indiana, pp. 12, 21, 34, 86, 94, 105, 108;
Reproduced from the Collections of the Library of Congress, pp. 4, 29,
45, 52, 68, 74, 90; National Archives and Records Administration,
pp. 10, 101.

Cover Illustration: Photo courtesy Eugene V. Debs Foundation, Terre
Haute, Indiana (Background); Courtesy Taminent Institute Library,
reproduced from the *Dictionary of American Portraits* (Debs Portrait).

CONTENTS

Eugene V. Debs

1

DEBS MAKES A SPEECH

Shortly after lunch on June 16, 1918, a group of Ohio socialists arrived at the Courtland Hotel in downtown Canton. They had a simple but important mission. Their job was to welcome Eugene V. Debs, the popular leader of the Socialist Party of America. Then, they would escort him across town to Nimisilla Park, where he was to speak before the party's state convention. Debs had given many fiery speeches over the last forty years, and people were looking forward to hearing his speech that day. Little did they know that it would become one of the most famous protest speeches in American history.

Debs the Person

Debs was one of the most important figures in the history of American labor. As a young man he had worked as a railroad fireman, shoveling the coal that kept the steam locomotives running. But he had devoted most of his adult life to making life better for working-class people and their families. His desire to improve things for the working class had led him to become a socialist.

Debs's work was his life. He had no interest in money or the fine things that money can buy. Most

Capitalism and Socialism

Modern people have organized their societies under two major economic systems: capitalism and socialism. Under capitalism, the means of production—like factories, farms, and railroads—are owned privately. Their owners run them to make a profit. Part of the profit they keep and spend on themselves. Another part is paid to their workers in wages. Under socialism, the means of production are owned by society. The government runs them and then distributes the profits to the people.

Generally speaking, people in socialist countries make less money than people in capitalist countries. However, they receive better public services like education, housing, and health care. Capitalist countries have more rich people, but they have more poor people, too.[1]

of his friends were either fellow socialists or labor leaders. He had no children, and he spent little time with his wife. Instead, he spent most of his time on the road, traveling from one meeting to the next, speaking about socialism. He gave away much of his money and many personal possessions, including his clothing and watch, to anyone he thought needed them more than he did.[2] Although most Americans thought he was strange, many working people adored him. He was one of the few people who devoted his life to improving the lives of workers and their families.

At sixty-two years of age, Debs was in good physical shape. Tall and lean, he could still stand up as straight as a much younger man. By the middle of a good speech, however, his lanky frame was usually hunched over. When he spoke, he gestured vigorously with the bony fingers of his large hands. His piercing eyes riveted his listeners, and his voice rang out strong and clear. Sometimes, he got so carried away that the veins would bulge from his large head as if they would burst.

The Day of the Speech

The weather was hotter than usual for a summer day in Canton. Debs insisted on wearing a jacket, vest, and tie anyway. He greeted his welcoming committee warmly, and they set out for the park.

On the way, Debs stopped at the Stark County Workhouse. This was the local jail for Canton and the surrounding countryside. In the jail were three Ohio socialists. They had been locked up for violating the Espionage Act of 1917. This act made it a federal crime to speak out against American involvement in World War I. The three men had broken the law by trying to convince young men not to register for the draft. The draft was established by Congress as a way of selecting young men for required military service.

The brief visit with his three jailed friends energized Debs. Afterwards, he briskly strolled the short distance to the park. He joked and laughed as he made his way through the friendly crowd of more than one thousand socialists and curious onlookers. Then, he stepped up to the podium and began to speak.[3]

Debs Attacks World War I

First, he thanked the cheering crowd for its enthusiastic welcome. Then he attacked the federal government's effort to silence the critics of its war program. The government had jailed his three friends, he said, for exercising their First Amendment right to freedom of speech. According to him, this meant that during his speech he would have to be "exceedingly careful, prudent, as to what I say, and even more careful and prudent as to how I say it."[4] This remark made much of the crowd laugh. Many people there had heard Debs speak before. They knew that once he got to talking, his remarks would be anything but careful and prudent.

Next, Debs attacked those Americans who approved of the government's efforts to silence its critics. Throughout history, he said, governments had appealed to patriotism to get people to fight in wars that should not have been fought. He called the owners of the factories that were making weapons and ammunition "greedy, profit-seeking exploiters" who were sacrificing the lives of soldiers just to make millions of "bloodstained dollars." Then, he attacked President Woodrow Wilson. Debs thought that Wilson was the one most responsible for involving the United States in the war.[5]

Wilson had proclaimed that the United States fought to make the world safe for democracy. Debs disagreed. Instead, he declared, the war was about conquest and plunder, like all wars. During the Middle Ages, he claimed, the nobles had declared war on each other. Then they had sent out their serfs to do the fighting. When the wars ended, he said, the serfs had died while the nobles profited from the spoils of war. It would be the same in this war, too, he declared. In fact, it was already working out that way. By the time of Debs's speech, millions

In New York City, young men are sworn into the Marines in 1918 after being drafted. Eugene V. Debs argued that most of the men who fought in World War I were from the working class.

of European soldiers and civilians had died in the war, and battles were still raging across the Atlantic. Meanwhile, the manufacturers of war supplies—Debs called them the "barons of Wall Street"—had made millions of dollars on sales to the governments fighting the war.[6]

Debs then attacked the way the United States had gotten into the war. He claimed that the working class, which furnished the soldiers, had never been asked if the United States should enter the war. Instead, he said, the ruling class had told the working class, "Yours not to reason why; yours but to do and die." If the working class had been asked to fight, he was convinced it would not have agreed.[7]

Debs was a great orator, or speaker. By this point in his speech, he had the crowd cheering. However, he had said some things that were not entirely true. For example, the feudal lords of the Middle Ages did fight one another. It was their job and the job of their knights, not the serfs, to wage war. Also, the decision to involve the United States in World War I was not made solely by President Wilson. It was also made by Congress, which had been elected by the American people.

But Debs was correct about several things. During World War I, it was mostly the working class of the world who were dying on the battlefields, not the wealthy. Instead, wealthy people directed the big companies that made millions of dollars by manufacturing weapons and ammunition. He was also correct when he accused the government of prosecuting the working class for exercising their First Amendment right to freedom of speech. All his three jailed friends had done, he said, was "reason why" out loud.

Debs Preaches Socialism

The rest of Debs's speech was about socialism. Debs believed that one day it would win out over capitalism. He believed that socialism had the power to improve the standard of living of most people. This was because a socialist government would distribute a larger share of the profits that big companies made to the workers. He also believed that capitalism encouraged greed, which started wars in general and

Debs and his unique speaking style got the crowds cheering in Canton, Ohio.

World War I in particular. By replacing capitalism with socialism, working-class people and their families could become more than "slaves and cannon fodder," Debs reasoned. Socialism, said Debs, promoted the good of the society, not just the good of wealthy individuals.[8]

Debs also praised the Bolsheviks. The Bolsheviks were Russian socialists who had overthrown the czar in 1917. Then, they made peace with Germany and Austria, Russia's enemies in World War I. He issued a rousing call to his listeners to play a more active role in the socialist movement. He asked them to recruit their friends, neighbors, and coworkers into the Socialist Party.[9]

Also in the crowd were spies working for the U. S. Justice Department. While Debs was speaking and the crowd was cheering, the spies busily scribbled down as much of his speech as they could. The Socialist Party of America had condemned the war and called on Americans to oppose it. For this reason, the Justice Department had been spying on all socialist meetings. They continued to spy on socialists until the end of World War I.

The spies turned their notes in to Edwin S. Wertz, the United States district attorney for northern Ohio. Wertz sent copies of the notes to his superiors in Washington, D. C. The notes were studied by Thomas W. Gregory, the United States attorney general. He told Wertz that the speech probably violated the Espionage Act. The case was not a strong one, however, and he advised Wertz not to prosecute Debs for just one speech. Wertz ignored Gregory, who showed little interest in the whole episode. Wertz believed that an Ohio jury would convict Debs. On June 29, 1918, Wertz got a federal grand jury to indict Debs on ten counts of violating the Espionage Act. Debs was arrested the following day. His trial was set for September 9, 1918, in Cleveland.[10]

2

WORKING ON THE RAILROAD

Eugene Victor Debs, called Gene as a child, was born on November 5, 1855, in Terre Haute, Indiana. His parents, Daniel and Marguerite, were from the city of Colmar in Alsace, a region in eastern France. In 1849, Daniel and Marguerite came to the United States and got married. For a while, they lived in New York City and then Cincinnati, Ohio. In 1851, they moved to Terre Haute.

Over the next four years, Daniel worked for several different employers. One of his jobs involved handling butchered hogs in a pork-packing plant. The hogs weighed more than five hundred pounds and it was hard for him to lift them. Later, he got a

Throughout his life, Eugene V. Debs would visit many cities in his native Midwest.

job laying heavy wooden ties for the Terre Haute & Indianapolis Railroad.

Daniel was not a large man. After four years of working twelve hours a day, six days a week, his health failed. He could no longer do hard physical labor like lifting hogs and laying ties.

In 1855, Marguerite did something that saved the family from starving. She withdrew their life savings and opened a small grocery store in the front room of their house. The store was a big success. Five years later, the Debses opened a bigger grocery store in downtown Terre Haute. By this time, Gene and his siblings—Louise, Eugenie, Theodore, Emma, and Marie—had been born.[1]

Debs's Boyhood

As a boy, Gene Debs did most of the things that other boys in Terre Haute did. He went hunting with his father. He swam, fished, and flew kites with his friends. He hiked through the woods and got into trouble around the house with his younger brother, Theodore. Like many little brothers, Theodore adored his big brother.

Gene was sent to a private school because Daniel Debs did not think the public school was any good. Gene got bored with school; too much reading, writing, and arithmetic, he thought.[2] However, he greatly enjoyed being read to by his father. Every

Sunday night after dinner, Daniel Debs would read to his children. Mostly, he read from the works of the great French and German authors. Gene's favorite was Victor Hugo's *Les Miserables*, the story of a French man who is almost destroyed by poverty but saved by friendship and love.[3]

Debs Goes to Work

As soon as Gene was old enough, he began helping his parents in their store. As he grew older, he began waiting on customers. Sometimes, his parents would leave him in charge of the store.

Gene could have taken over the family store one day and become a well-to-do businessman in Terre Haute. But he was as bored with the grocery business as he was with school. He had many arguments with his parents about his future. They finally admitted that Gene was a bad businessman. Gene often gave customers more groceries than they paid

This portrait was taken in 1870, when Eugene V. Debs was a teenager.

for. Sometimes he gave groceries to people on credit, even though he knew they could not pay their bills. With his parents' permission, he dropped out of high school at the end of his freshman year. At the age of fourteen, he went to work on his own.[4]

Daniel Debs had a friend named Pierre Solomon. Solomon worked in the maintenance shops of the Vandalia Railroad, formerly the Terre Haute & Indianapolis. Solomon got Gene a job with the Vandalia as an unskilled laborer for fifty cents per

The Importance of Railroads

Railroads were the most important means of transportation in the nineteenth century. By the end of the century, railroads hauled most of the interstate passengers and freight. Nearly every town had a station. Larger businesses had their own sidings where freight cars could be loaded and unloaded.

Railroads were also the largest industries of the nineteenth century. A modest-sized railroad employed thousands of people. It also spent millions of dollars each year on supplies and equipment. Railroads were the nation's largest consumers of iron, steel, coal, and petroleum (oil) products.

The nation's economy depended on railroads. Railroads stimulated business by delivering raw materials and manufactured goods. However, they also consumed huge quantities of these items themselves.

day. Gene's first job was to clean the grease from the undersides of locomotives. The degreaser left his hands raw and bleeding. His next job was to scrape paint from locomotives. This meant he had to buy his own paint-scraping tool. The tool cost one dollar, or two day's wages.

After several months of hard labor, Gene proved his worth as a workingman. He was promoted to a crew that painted all the switches between Terre Haute and Indianapolis. This was a stretch of about seventy miles, and sometimes he had to spend the night away from home. Once the switches were painted, he was assigned to paint stripes and letters on locomotives.[5]

Debs Becomes a Fireman

About a year later, just before Christmas Day, 1871, Gene caught a lucky break. The fireman for the switch engine that handled Terre Haute's freight yard came to work drunk. The engineer convinced Gene to take the drunken man's place for just one shift. Soon, Gene was working as a full-time fireman. The new job was not easy. The fireman kept the fire burning in a steam locomotive's boiler. To do this, he had to shovel coal from the tender (the car behind the locomotive) to the firebox in the locomotive's cab. A fireman might shovel several tons of coal just on one trip. His back always hurt

One of Debs's first jobs was as a painter in the railroad yards. Here he sits (bottom left) with the rest of his crew.

and his muscles were always sore. He mostly worked out in the open in all kinds of weather, so he froze in the winter, roasted in the summer, and got drenched whenever it rained.

Being a fireman was not all bad, though. Riding the rails from Terre Haute to Indianapolis meant lots of fresh air. It also meant a change of scenery from the cold, damp maintenance shop. As a skilled laborer, he got more respect from his fellow railroaders and from the general public. Best of all, he received a raise, to one dollar per day. He used the extra money to pay his tuition to business college. The boy who hated school was now going to night school to study railroad business and accounting.[6]

Debs Gets Laid Off

Eugene Debs worked as a fireman for the Vandalia for another two years. Then, the Panic of 1873 occurred. This economic depression resulted in a major loss of business for many American companies. Thousands of railroad workers, including Debs, lost their jobs. Unable to find work in Terre Haute, he could no longer afford to go to business college.

Skilled and Unskilled Labor

During the nineteenth century, there were two types of workers: skilled and unskilled. A skilled laborer was anyone who had to have special knowledge to do the job. A fireman was considered a skilled laborer because he had to know how to keep the fire burning in the firebox. Unskilled laborers did work that required no special knowledge. This work was usually either heavy, dirty, or difficult, like degreasing the underside of a locomotive.

Skilled laborers were relatively hard to find, so they were paid more. They were also treated with more respect than unskilled laborers. Unskilled laborers could be found just about everywhere. They were looked down upon by employers and the general population alike because they made very little money.

He dropped out of school and traveled to St. Louis, Missouri. When he got there, he was shocked to see how many people were out of work. He was even more shocked to see the miserable conditions in which working-class people and their families were forced to live because they were out of work. These conditions were similar to some of the scenes in *Les Miserables*, a favorite book from his childhood. The hero is an escaped convict who struggles to live an honest life in spite of the overwhelming prejudices of a cruel society.

Debs searched and searched for a job. Finally, he was hired as a substitute night fireman on a yard switcher—a type of train locomotive that is used for moving railroad cars. He worked off and on for a year and struggled to make ends meet. He was homesick and broke. He also had few friends. In his spare time, he studied his old college business books. He also reread the classics his father had once read to him.[7]

Meanwhile, Debs's mother was trying to convince him that working on the railroad was too dangerous. In order to make money during the depression, railroads ran equipment that was poorly maintained. Unsafe locomotives and railroad cars caused many accidents involving workers. Many of these accidents were reported in the newspapers. After a coworker fell under a locomotive and was crushed to death, Debs decided to take his mother's advice and quit his job.

In 1874, Debs left his job as a fireman and returned to Terre Haute. Once again, his father found him a job through a friend. Herman Hulman was co-owner of Hulman & Cox, the wholesale grocery firm that supplied the Debses' store. Hulman hired Debs to work as a billing clerk.[8]

Debs retired as an active fireman at the age of nineteen. Never again would he do hard physical labor for a living. However, he never forgot his experiences as a workingman. For the rest of his life, he would be motivated by these experiences to try to make life better for the working class.

3

THE BROTHERHOOD OF LOCOMOTIVE FIREMEN

Debs hated the wholesale grocery business, but not because the work was too hard. All he had to do was keep track of what went in and out of the warehouse, then bill customers for what they had ordered. If anything, it was too easy for someone who was used to the rough-and-tumble life of a fireman.

Debs missed the physical activity, the practical jokes, and the excitement of working on the railroad. In his spare time, he would go down to the yard and hang around the maintenance shop. Sometimes, he would go to the saloons where the railroadmen drank.[1]

Debs Joins the BLF

In early 1875, Debs became a charter member of the Vigo Lodge of the Brotherhood of Locomotive Firemen (BLF). He almost did not get to join because the BLF recruiter was reluctant to sign up a grocery clerk. The other firemen assured the recruiter that Debs was still one of them in spirit.

The BLF was a mutual aid society, not a union. It offered firemen affordable life and accident insurance. It also provided a lodge where firemen could socialize. Otherwise, it offered very little. The BLF did not try to win higher wages or better working conditions for firemen. Its constitution prohibited members from striking, an effective tool working-class people have against their employers. Its motto was "Benevolence, Sobriety, and Industry." Its members pledged to help one another during hard times. They promised not to drink alcohol. They promised to give a fair day's work for a fair day's pay.[2]

At the Vigo Lodge's first meeting, Debs was elected recording secretary. He took the minutes, or notes on the meeting's events, of each business meeting. He also corresponded with other chapters and the national office. He was delighted to be in the BLF because now he could play fireman without having to work as one.

Many firemen did not share Debs's delight with the BLF. Old members began to drop out faster than new ones could be brought in. The problem was that working on the railroad had changed since the Panic of 1873.

Before the Panic, most railroads thought their employees were valuable assets. They tried to pay their workers well. They also looked out for their workers' safety by maintaining the locomotives and cars. During and after the Panic, railroads had to cut costs wherever they could. This meant running unsafe equipment. It also meant working their employees longer hours and paying them less. What firemen needed now was more than insurance and a social club. They needed a union to fight for better wages and working conditions.[3]

The Railroad Strike of 1877

In the summer of 1877, the Pennsylvania and the Baltimore & Ohio railroads announced a wage cut. Many engineers and firemen protested by walking off the job. Within days, the strike spread across the country. It was the first national strike in U. S. history. In most places, the strike remained peaceful. In Pittsburgh, Pennsylvania, however, an angry mob took over the Pennsylvania Railroad's main shop. Then the mob set fire to hundreds of locomotives and freight cars. The U. S. Army and the state militia were called in to restore order. More than one hundred strikers were shot to death, and hundreds more were wounded.[4]

Most of the BLF's members now realized that the relationship between railroad workers and railroad companies had changed. Before the strike, the workers thought they were partners. Now they realized that they were enemies. They also realized that they needed to fight for safer working conditions and decent pay. The BLF showed little interest in these things, so many members quit.

To make matters worse, most railroad companies considered the BLF to be a union. When the railroads began firing railroad workers who belonged to unions, they also fired BLF members. Many BLF members gave up their memberships to save their jobs.

Debs Saves the BLF

By 1880, the BLF was in serious trouble. Its national membership was less than thirteen hundred, and it was six thousand dollars in debt.[5] The brotherhood might have died if Debs had not given it new life. Since 1877, he had performed well as grand marshall of the BLF. He had also served as assistant editor of the *Locomotive Firemen's Magazine*, the BLF's monthly newsletter. In 1880, Grand Master Frank Arnold and Grand Instructor Sam Stevens, the

HARPER'S WEEKLY.

JOURNAL OF CIVILIZATION

Vol. XXI.—No. 1076.]   NEW YORK, SATURDAY, AUGUST 11, 1877.   [WITH A SUPPLEMENT. PRICE TEN CENTS.

Entered according to Act of Congress, in the Year 1877, by Harper & Brothers, in the Office of the Librarian of Congress, at Washington.

The Railroad Strike of 1877, called the Great Strike, became violent in Baltimore. This August 11, 1877 cover of Harper's Weekly *depicts the Sixth Maryland Regiment clashing with strikers.*

Railroad Companies and Unions

A union is a group of employees in the same company or industry who band together to gain better working conditions and wages. An effective weapon a union has is the strike. Striking workers do not go to work, so the company gets nothing done. If the company cannot break, or stop, the strike, it has to give in to the union to get the strikers to come back to work.

Sometimes, a company can break a strike by hiring strikebreakers, also known as "scabs." Strikebreakers are unemployed workers who are willing to take the place of strikers. Usually, strikebreakers are not as skilled as the workers they replace, but they are often good enough to get the work done.

Railroad companies used strikebreakers, but they did not like to do so. Railroad jobs required more skill than most other jobs. Most scabs did not have the necessary skills to run a train. Strikebreakers wrecked many trains, not deliberately but by accident, and a train wreck was expensive. To avoid strikes, railroad companies tried to keep out unions. Many railroads fired any employee who joined one.

BLF's top elected officials, asked Debs to help them save the BLF. They wanted him to take over as editor of the magazine and as national secretary-treasurer. This would put Debs in charge of the BLF's day-to-day operations.[6]

At first, Debs refused. A year earlier, he had been elected city clerk of Terre Haute. He thought he might have a brilliant political career ahead of him. Also, he was not sure about the brotherhood's future or its ability to pay his salary.[7] Arnold and Stevens convinced Debs that they would recruit lots of new members. The initiation dues from these members would pay off the BLF's debts. The dues would also cover its expenses, including Debs's salary.

Debs took the positions. He thought the BLF could still serve firemen. He disliked unions because most of them had an anti-company attitude. He disliked strikes because he thought they did strikers more harm than good. But he also knew that the BLF must do more for its members than offer insurance and social activities. He still wanted the BLF to encourage firemen to work hard and to respect the profits and property of the railroad companies. But he also saw that the brotherhood must begin to negotiate with the railroad companies for better wages and working conditions.[8]

As the new editor and secretary-treasurer, Debs quickly gave BLF members something to cheer about. A local BLF official had been thrown out of the office of a Pennsylvania Railroad vice-president. The official complained to Debs about the insult. Debs immediately went to the vice-president to demand an apology. He cursed Debs and refused to apologize. Debs cursed him back and refused to leave. For an hour they cursed and screamed at each other.[9] Eventually, Debs made the vice-president understand that the BLF was not a union. Debs convinced him that BLF members wanted to work with the railroads, not against them. The vice-president apologized and promised to treat the BLF with respect in the future. It was a promise that he and his company kept.

Word of Debs's victory spread through the ranks of the nation's firemen. They appreciated Debs's ability to command respect from a railroad as large as the Pennsylvania. They began to join the BLF in greater numbers. By 1882, Arnold and Stevens had recruited enough new firemen to boost membership to almost five thousand. As planned, their initiation dues settled the BLF's outstanding debts and paid for its day-to-day operations.[10]

Debs's term as city clerk expired in 1884. As soon as it had, he joined Arnold and Stevens as a BLF recruiter. The work of forming new lodges was frustrating. The Pennsylvania Railroad respected the brotherhood, but most other railroads still considered it to be a union. They continued to fire anyone who joined it. In many towns, Debs could not find firemen brave enough to start a new lodge.

To make matters worse, the BLF did not have enough money for Debs's travel expenses. When he could, he talked a friendly train crew into letting him ride in the locomotive cab. When he could not, he hopped into an empty boxcar and rode for free. He spent many nights in cabooses, maintenance sheds, and in the homes of friendly railroad workers. He often ate whatever they were kind enough to feed him. He usually returned to his BLF duties in Terre Haute hungry, sick, and exhausted. He rested for a short while and caught up with his official BLF duties. Then he was ready to make another recruiting trip. Eventually, his hard work and sacrifice paid off. By 1890, the BLF had twenty thousand members. Meanwhile, the *Locomotive Firemen's Magazine* had become a respected voice of all railroad workers, not just firemen, and it sold thirty-three thousand copies each month.[11]

Debs Gets Married

Debs had little time for a social life, but he did not care. Most of his friends were members of the BLF. He thoroughly enjoyed making new friends with firemen across the country. As for getting married, most young women struck him as being frivolous, thinking only of new clothes and fancy parties. Then he met Kate Metzel, a friend of his sister, Marie.

Kate was a serious young woman. Debs could talk to her about his work with the BLF and his dreams for its future. In 1885, they were married. They then toured the big cities of the East, including New York City and Washington, D. C. By the

This photo of Eugene Debs (left) and his wife Kate was taken later in life. Their nephew sits in the parlor of their home with them.

time they got back to Terre Haute, they had spent all their money. They were too happy with each other to care. They rented a three-room apartment and furnished it with gifts from BLF lodges across the country.[12]

Not long after the honeymoon, Debs left on another recruiting trip. Over the next forty years, he spent little time with his wife. They never had any children because Kate was unable to get pregnant. At one point, she thought about going to a clinic in Louisville, Kentucky, that promised to help women who were unable to have children. Her mother advised against it, though. She thought the operation was too dangerous, and she convinced Kate to "let well enough alone."[13]

While her husband was on the road, Kate kept busy by doing housework and reading. Four years after their wedding, she convinced Debs to build a fancy house in a fashionable neighborhood in Terre Haute. It was much larger than they needed, but cleaning and decorating it gave Kate something to do. Later, she took in her mother, as well as a nephew, Oscar, whose parents had died. Her mother and nephew helped take the place of the stay-at-home husband and children she longed for.[14]

The Wabash Strike

In 1885, the Wabash Railroad cut the wages of its employees by 10 percent. In protest, Wabash railroad workers walked off the job. The strike had been called by the Knights of Labor, an organization for working-class people in general. It was supported by the Brotherhood of Locomotive Engineers (BLE). Several BLF lodges also walked out, even though their constitution prohibited them from striking. By supporting each other, the three groups got the Wabash to cancel the pay cut. They also won the right to belong to unions.

The strike's success electrified railroadmen across the United States. At their convention later that year, BLF delegates repealed the no-strike clause in their constitution. They also went on record as belonging to a union, not a mutual aid society or brotherhood. Debs was instructed to work out a national alliance with the BLE. The BLF hoped that the alliance would help it win more victories like the Wabash Strike.[15]

Debs wanted to ally with the BLE. He hoped that the threat of a joint strike by engineers and firemen would make strikes unnecessary, since a railroad could hardly operate without them. Over the next three years, the two brotherhoods worked together. They negotiated successfully with four smaller railroads. In each case, the railroad workers got what they wanted without having to strike.

After these victories, Debs began calling for a federation of all the railroad brotherhoods. While recruiting for the BLF, he had helped to form brotherhoods for brakemen, switchmen, and sleeping car porters, as well. Now he wanted all railroad workers to unite. Together, they could win better wages and working conditions without striking.[16]

The Burlington Strike

In 1888, the BLF and BLE went on strike against the Chicago, Burlington & Quincy Railroad. The

Who Does What on a Railroad?

Railroads of the nineteenth century needed many skilled laborers to operate safely and profitably. Engineers drove the steam locomotives that pulled the trains. Firemen kept the steam up by shoveling coal into the fireboxes and putting water into the boilers. Brakemen made the trains stop. Switchmen coupled and uncoupled the cars. They also operated the turnouts that switched trains from one track to the next. Conductors kept track of which cars were headed where. They also told the engineers and brakemen when and where to stop. Sleeping car porters took care of passengers on sleeping cars.

Burlington, as it was called, was the biggest railroad they had faced to date. Once again, the issue was a wage cut. The brotherhoods had tried to negotiate, but the company refused.

Unlike the four smaller railroads, the Burlington fought the strike. It brought in unemployed railroad workers from around the country. These strike-breakers managed to keep the Burlington's trains running on schedule. However, they were a bit rusty, and they caused several expensive train wrecks. The Burlington tried to get a federal judge to issue an injunction, or court order, against the strike. The company told the judge that the strike interfered with the delivery of the U. S. mail, which was a federal crime. Peter M. Arthur, the leader of the BLE, got scared that he might go to jail if he defied the injunction. He ordered the BLE to end their strike even before the injunction was issued. Without the support of the BLE, the BLF could not hope to win. They went back to work, too. In 1889, after almost a full year of striking, the walkout ended. The strikers had won nothing.[17]

The failure of the Burlington strike convinced Debs more than ever of the need for a federation of railroad brotherhoods. It also convinced the BLF. At its national convention in 1888, the delegates asked Debs to talk with the engineers, conductors, brake-men, and switchmen about forming an alliance.

A National Railroad Federation

Debs got the best response from the brotherhoods of the brakemen and switchmen. He had helped start both brotherhoods, and their members thought of him as a founding father. In June 1889, firemen, brakemen, and switchmen met in Chicago. They formed the Supreme Council of the United Orders of Railway Employees. Over the next year, the Supreme Council helped railroadmen win better working conditions and wages from railroads across the country without striking.

Then, in 1890, the brakemen decided to increase their influence by recruiting more members to their organization. They changed their name to the Brotherhood of Railroad Trainmen (BRT) and began recruiting switchmen as well as brakemen. The BRT ignored the outraged complaints of the switchmen, whose turf was being invaded. For two years, the Supreme Council was crippled by the feud between the two groups. Several attempts to get the BRT to stop recruiting switchmen failed. Finally, in 1892 the Supreme Council expelled the BRT. It soon became clear that the Supreme Council could not be effective without the BRT. It was dissolved later that year.[18]

Despite the Supreme Council's failure, Debs remained committed to the cause of railroad workers. That commitment had changed, though, since he had joined the BLF in 1875. Then, he had believed that railroad workers and companies could work together for their common good. Now, he believed that the workers would have to fight to get fair treatment from the companies. Before, he was opposed to strikes because he thought they did not work. Now, he knew that the threat of a strike was the only method that did work. He believed that a single union could best represent the interests of railroad workers across the country. Creating such a union became the focus of the next phase of his life.

4

THE AMERICAN RAILWAY UNION

By 1892, Debs had been working for several years to create one union for American railroad workers. The failure of the Supreme Council showed him that the brotherhoods could not see past their own special interests. One brotherhood might not honor a strike called by another brotherhood. This meant that the new union would have to be organized without the brotherhoods. He knew that less than 25 percent of the nation's railroad workers belonged to the brotherhoods. The main reason was that the dues were too high. He figured that he could easily recruit enough members from the remaining 75 percent to make the new union work.[1]

Debs Leaves the BLF

Debs began planning for a future that did not include the BLF. First, he founded E.V. Debs Publishing Company. The company printed and sold books about railroading, and he hoped it would bring in enough money to support his wife and himself. Then, at the BLF's next national convention, he announced his resignation as secretary-treasurer and editor.[2]

The great majority of the BLF's members did not agree with Debs's new approach to unionizing railroad workers. But they admired and respected him anyway. For years, Debs had traveled among them and organized them. He had shared their lives in a special way, even though he had only been a fireman for a short time. He had loaned them money without expecting to be repaid. Several times, he had given a fireman the shirt or coat off his back. As secretary-treasurer, he had written the insurance checks that kept them and their loved ones from starving or being evicted from their homes.

Because they respected him, they begged him to stay. They offered him a big raise and an all-expenses-paid vacation to Europe if he would stay. But Debs knew that his future was not with the BLF. He wanted to build a new kind of union that the brotherhoods could not yet accept. In the end, they worked out a compromise. Debs stepped down as secretary-treasurer, but he agreed to continue as editor of the *Locomotive Firemen's Magazine*.[3]

Birth of the American Railway Union

Over the next year, Debs came up with a constitution for his railroad workers' union. He unveiled his plan at a meeting in June 1893 in Chicago. At the meeting were fifty railroad workers who also wanted to unite all railroad workers in one union. Among them were the leaders of the Brotherhood of Railroad Conductors and the Brotherhood of Railway Carmen.

During this meeting, the American Railway Union (ARU) was born. Under its bylaws, the individual crafts, like firemen and engineers, would manage their own affairs. All members regardless of craft, however, were required to walk out together during a strike.

The ARU promised to improve the wages and working conditions of all railroad workers. It pledged to work for legislation that bettered the lot of railroad workers. It made plans to provide inexpensive accident and life insurance, and to publish a newsletter and magazine. To attract members, dues were kept low—one dollar to join, and one dollar per year to stay in. Debs was chosen as the ARU's first president.[4]

The railroad brotherhoods opposed the ARU, but railroad workers joined it anyway. In some cases, entire locals of the Railway Carmen and Switchmen left their brotherhoods and joined the ARU. In other cases, individual firemen, engineers, conductors, brakemen, switchmen, and sleeping car porters quit their brotherhoods and joined the ARU. But most of the ARU's members came from the group that Debs most wanted to organize. These were the railroad workers who had never belonged to a brotherhood. These men flocked to the ARU in numbers that surprised even Debs. In three weeks, the ARU established thirty-four locals and signed up more than four thousand members. By the end of the year, the ARU had more than eighty locals.[5]

In 1894, the ARU ran into a major challenge. The nation was in the middle of another depression, the Panic of 1893. Thousands of companies, including hundreds of railroads, had fallen on hard times. The Union Pacific Railroad had filed for bankruptcy in the federal court in Cheyenne, Wyoming. This meant that the court had to approve all its business decisions. To cut costs, the railroad declared a major wage cut for its workers. One of the judges issued an injunction prohibiting the workers from striking over the wage cut. Debs met with the court's judges and convinced them to cancel the wage cut and the injunction. This was a major victory for the ARU,

HARPER'S WEEKLY

A JOURNAL OF CIVILIZATION

Vol. XXXVIII.—No. 1960.
Copyright, 1894, by Harper & Brothers.
All Rights Reserved.

NEW YORK, SATURDAY, JULY 14, 1894.

TEN CENTS A COPY.
FOUR DOLLARS A YEAR.

KING DEBS.

This July 14, 1894 cover of Harper's Weekly *depicts Eugene V. Debs as "King Debs" because of the strength of the American Railway Union that he started.*

and it led thousands more railroadmen to join the new union.

The Great Northern Strike

The ARU's next challenge came a month later. This time the problem involved the Great Northern Railroad. Once again the problem was a wage cut, and once again Debs threw himself into the middle of the situation. When the Great Northern refused to negotiate with the ARU, the union called a strike.

Debs went to St. Paul, Minnesota, headquarters of the Great Northern, to manage the strike personally. He wanted to make sure that the different crafts stood together so that no freight or passenger trains would run. He also wanted to make sure the mail trains kept moving. During the Burlington Strike, a federal judge had threatened to jail railroad workers who refused to handle mail trains. Debs also wanted to make sure that no violence was done to people or property. As long as the mail moved and the strike stayed peaceful, troops could not be called in to break the strike as they had in 1877.

The strikers were careful to follow Debs's instructions. The mail kept moving, the strike stayed peaceful, and the troops stayed away. After several weeks, the Great Northern realized it had been beaten. The company agreed to submit the wage cut to an arbitration board. The board agreed with the company that wages had to be reduced. But it allowed a cut of less than 2 1/2 percent instead of the 25 percent that the company wanted.[6]

Once again, the ARU had won a major victory, and once again thousands of railroad workers joined up. At the union's convention later that year, the ARU had 465 local chapters and more than 150,000 members. By comparison, the membership of all the railroad brotherhoods combined was less than one hundred thousand.[7]

The success of the strike against the Great Northern was the high point of the ARU's existence. It was also the highlight of Debs's career as a railroad organizer. He believed it marked the

Arbitration

When two people or parties cannot agree to something, they sometimes agree to let a third party arbitrate, or reach a decision, for them. Sometimes, the decision is made by one person. Other times, it is made by a number of people called a board. It all depends on who the disagreeing parties choose. Either way, the third party is usually knowledgeable about the situation. The third party also has no personal stake in the outcome. Submitting something to arbitration usually results in a fair decision. Neither party gets everything it wants, but both sides usually get enough to be satisfied.

beginning of the end of the conflict between the railroads and railroad workers. He felt sure that now the companies knew that the workers would stand together during a strike.

Debs was wrong. The success of the Great Northern Strike marked only the beginning of the end of the ARU. Many of the union's members had little experience in organized labor. They mistakenly thought they now could win a strike against any railroad company. The strike did not impress the railroad companies with the ARU's strength. Instead, the companies were determined to destroy the ARU.

The Pullman Strike

While the ARU was celebrating its victory over the Great Northern, a bigger strike was brewing in Chicago. This one involved the Pullman Palace Car Company. Pullman manufactured sleeping cars and operated them on the various railroads. Once again the issue was wage cuts, in some cases as much as 50 percent. When workers tried to negotiate, Pullman refused. The company also refused to lower rents on the company-owned houses that most of its employees lived in. Many Pullman workers soon found themselves unable to pay their rent.

Desperate, the Pullman workers decided to strike. Almost all of Pullman's forty-three hundred employees walked off the job. About one third of the strikers had recently joined the ARU. They appealed to the union to support their strike.[8]

Debs and the other leaders of the ARU did not want to get involved in the Pullman Strike. They were still tired from the Great Northern Strike, which had ended just a few weeks earlier. Also, there were some problems that most of the ARU's members did not understand. When the union fought the Union Pacific and the Great Northern, it did so in the Midwest and the West. This is where most of the ARU's locals were. Pullman operated sleeping cars on just about every railroad in the country, including the South and the East where the ARU had few members. While striking against Union Pacific and Great Northern, the union only had to fight one railroad at a time. Pullman was supported by the General Managers Association (GMA). This group represented the twenty-four railroads that ran trains in or through Chicago, where Pullman's factories were. Although thousands of railroadmen had recently joined the union, the ARU had spent most of its money fighting the Union Pacific and the Great Northern. It had very little left to use against Pullman.

Debs and the other leaders tried to convince the ARU's members to stay out of the strike against Pullman. Instead, the leaders tried to get Pullman to submit the matter to arbitration. But Pullman refused, and the members felt confident after their victories over the Union Pacific and the Great Northern. Despite Debs's advice, the union voted to strike. Debs was instructed to tell Pullman that ARU members would boycott Pullman. This means that they would not handle trains that carried Pullman sleeping cars.[9]

The Pullman Strike ran into problems from the very beginning. Most of the ARU's one hundred fifty thousand members took part in the boycott. But the GMA brought in non-ARU employees from the South and East to work trains carrying Pullman cars, so the boycott had little effect.[10]

What Is a Boycott?

Refusing to do business with a person or company is called a boycott. Under United States law, it is perfectly legal for a group to refuse to buy the goods or services of a particular company. It is also legal to announce this intention to the world in the hope that others will join the boycott. It is illegal, however, to force someone else to join the boycott. Boycotters may demonstrate in front of a store, for example, but they may not prevent people from entering that store.

During the Pullman Strike, ARU members were entitled to refuse to handle Pullman cars. They were not allowed to prevent non-members from handling Pullman cars.

Then, the boycotters began stopping trains that carried Pullman cars. In and around Chicago, mail trains were delayed and railroad property was damaged. The damage and the delays gave the GMA an excuse to ask the government for help. The GMA demanded that federal marshals and troops be sent to Chicago to protect property and lives. Several witnesses later claimed that some of the destruction was ordered by the GMA as a way to make the ARU look bad. These witnesses also claimed that the railroads delayed their own trains, then blamed the delays on the boycotters so that troops would be called in.[11]

The GMA pressured the railroad brotherhoods to publicly declare their non-support for the boycott. Many of the brotherhoods had lost a lot of members to the ARU, so they did as the GMA asked. Most importantly, the GMA succeeded in getting the support of Richard Olney, the United States attorney general. He had been a railroad lawyer before being appointed attorney general by President Grover Cleveland, and he hated unions. As attorney general, he was in charge of the U. S. Justice Department. The department employed hundreds of the nation's best lawyers and could deputize as many marshals as it wanted.

GEORGE M. PULLMAN,
President of the Pullman Company.

SENATOR CUSHMAN K. DAVIS, OF MINNESOTA,
Senator of the Patriotic Telegram refusing to support Kyle's Resolution.

EUGENE V. DEBS,
President of the American Railway Union.

COMPLETE BLOCKADE OF FREIGHT AND PASSENGER CARS, JULY 3, 1894—CHICAGO AND NORTHWESTERN RAILROAD, NEAR HALSTED STREET

RECEIVING AND QUESTIONING APPLICANTS FOR APPOINTMENTS AS DEPUTIES AT THE MARSHALS OFFICE, CHICAGO

CHICAGO AND NORTHWESTERN RAILROAD ROUND-HOUSE, JULY 3, 1894—NO AN ENGINE MOVING

This photo depicts scenes from the railroad strikes in Chicago. At the top are George Pullman (left), Senator Cushman K. Davis of Minnesota (middle), and Eugene V. Debs. Davis was against the railroad companies. A blockade of railroad cars is seen in the second picture from the top.

The Federal Government Crushes the Strike

Olney figured out how to use the Sherman Antitrust Act against the ARU. This act had been passed in 1890 as a way to get rid of monopolies. Monopolies are large companies that control the market in a particular product or service. The Sherman Antitrust Act outlawed any group that tried to fix prices or interfere with interstate commerce in any way. Olney convinced the federal district court in Chicago that unions try to fix the price of labor by negotiating wages. He also convinced the court that the ARU was interfering with interstate commerce by refusing to handle Pullman cars.

The court issued an injunction against the ARU's leaders. The injunction ordered them to have nothing at all to do with the boycott. Olney convinced President Cleveland to send in twenty-five hundred federal troops and thousands of federal marshals to enforce the injunction.

As a Democrat, Cleveland had once been considered a friend of the working-class. He had been elected president in 1892. By 1894, he had realized that he had to have the backing of the Republicans in Congress if he wanted any of his programs to pass. Ever since the late 1860s, the Republican Party had championed the interests of big companies, including the railroads. Cleveland decided to do something to gain Republican support.

Meanwhile, the newspapers had gotten involved. They were making the boycotters look like a bunch of lawless rioters. In order to make himself look good to the business community and the general public, Cleveland did as Olney asked. He sent troops to Chicago to end the boycott. He claimed that the troops were needed to protect lives and property and to restore normal mail delivery.[12]

The federal injunction put the ARU in an impossible situation. Debs and the other leaders knew that if they continued to lead the boycott, they would be jailed for contempt of court. They also knew that if they stopped directing the boycott, then it would collapse. If this happened, then the ARU would not only lose the battle against Pullman. It would also be forced to disband because it could never call another strike again.

Debs was furious about the injunction. He did everything he could to get it cancelled. Unfortunately, there was little he could do. Even John P. Altgeld, the pro-union governor of Illinois and a Democrat, tried to use his influence with Cleveland to get the injunction cancelled. Cleveland ignored him, and the troops and marshals stayed. Debs tried to get the railroad brotherhoods, the Knights of Labor, and the American Federation of Labor to join the

Pullman Strike. But they refused to get involved in a losing battle. In the end, Debs and his fellow leaders chose to ignore the injunction.[13]

Then the boycott turned violent. In suburban Blue Island, the stockyards downtown, and the Panhandle yards in South Chicago, mobs attacked railroad property and set it on fire. They also insulted the troops and threw rocks at them. In return, the troops opened fire on the mobs. Over the next week, the troops killed thirty rioters and wounded almost one hundred.

A federal grand jury indicted Debs and the other ARU leaders for conspiracy to interfere with interstate commerce. They were arrested by federal marshals, jailed, and released on bond. Then they were arrested for violating the injunction against leading the boycott. This time, they refused bail and stayed in jail instead. Shortly thereafter, the Pullman Strike ended. Word that their leaders were in jail and that federal troops were killing railroad workers sent the boycotters back to work. Pullman cars were once again handled by ARU members as if nothing had ever happened.[14]

The ARU on Trial

Debs and his fellow leaders spent eight days in jail. Then, they were released on bond until their first trial in late 1894. At this trial, they were found guilty of contempt of court for ignoring the boycott. Debs was sentenced to six months in jail while the other six leaders got three months each. They appealed their convictions to the U. S. Supreme Court on the grounds that the injunction was unconstitutional.

Meanwhile, a federal commission appointed by President Cleveland investigated the Pullman Strike. It declared that the biggest part of the blame for the boycott fell on Pullman, not the ARU. It also found that the GMA had used illegal tactics to discredit the union. Nothing, however, was ever done about the commission's report.[15]

The trial for conspiring to interfere with interstate commerce began in Chicago in early 1895. For about a month, the union leaders' lawyers attacked the prosecution's case. Finally, the judge called a halt to the trial and let the leaders go free. But in the summer of 1895, the Supreme Court handed down its ruling. It declared that the lower court had every right to issue the injunction barring the ARU's leaders from participating in the strike. An injunction is not an official court decision. It is an order to cease and desist until such a decision can be made. In the lower court's opinion, the boycott had posed a real threat to the peace. The Supreme Court ruled that it had acted properly to halt the boycott until its merits could be debated in court. Debs and his fellow ARU leaders were ordered to serve their sentences.[16]

Debs and his comrades were sent to McHenry County Jail in Woodstock, Illinois. The jail only consisted of a few cells attached to the house of George Eckert, the county sheriff. He took a liking to the union leaders and let them out of their cells during the day. He even let them eat dinner with his family and play football in the street behind his house.

Debs spent much of his time in jail trying to keep the ARU alive. He read and answered hundreds of letters from union members wondering what to do next. He also gave interviews to reporters from around the country, hoping to keep the union in the minds of railroadmen. But his best efforts could not save the ARU. It had been crushed by the combined power of the railroad companies and the federal government. By the time he got out of jail in November 1895, the ARU was in desperate shape.[17]

Debs spent the next eighteen months touring the country. He tried to organize new locals and recruit new members. But it was too late to save the ARU. In order to destroy the union, the railroads had used a tactic known as blacklisting. Any railroadman who joined the ARU was fired, and his name was put on a "blacklist." The railroads shared their blacklists with each other. Anyone whose name was on one railroad's list would not get hired by any other railroad. Blacklisting kept many railroadmen from joining the ARU. It also forced many members to quit to save their jobs.

By June 1897, when the ARU held its last national convention, the union had only a few hundred members. It was clear that the ARU's time had come and gone, so the members voted to disband. Then, at the same meeting, they voted to create a new organization. The new organization was intended to help all working-class people, not just railroad workers. It was called the Social Democracy of America. By joining it, Debs became a socialist.[18]

5

FROM DEMOCRAT TO SOCIALIST

The failure of the Pullman Strike had convinced Debs that unions would never be treated fairly by railroad companies. He believed that the strike had failed because the federal government had backed the companies. When he got out of jail in November 1895, he realized that working-class people must get involved in politics. Their first goal would be to get the federal government to treat companies and unions the same.

Debs the Democrat

Even before he went to jail, Debs had gotten involved in politics. From 1879 to 1884, he was the city clerk of Terre Haute. In 1885, he was elected to the Indiana state legislature. He had considered himself a loyal Democrat because Democrats showed more interest in the problems of the working class than Republicans did. He changed his mind about being a Democrat during the Pullman Strike. President Cleveland, a Democrat, had used federal troops to help the railroad companies break up the strike. Cleveland's actions convinced Debs that neither the Democrats nor the Republicans had any interest in the working class. He began to look for a party that did.[1]

Debs the Populist

Debs turned his attention to the People's Party, better known today as the Populists. The Populists were mostly farmers and small, rural business-people. Like the working class, they were unhappy with the way big companies dominated American society.

Debs did not agree with everything the Populists wanted to do. But he believed they had good intentions toward the working class. At the ARU convention in 1894, he supported a resolution that endorsed working-class support for a third party. By the end of the Pullman Strike, he made it clear that he favored the Populists.

After the Pullman Strike, Debs tried to get the working-class to vote for the Populist candidates in

The Populists

Populists wanted the federal government to take greater control over American society. They wanted it to take over the railroads and the banks. That way, freight prices and interest rates could be lowered so that people could afford them. They also wanted the federal government to tax the incomes of wealthy businesspeople. At the time, only land and imported goods were taxed. This meant that farmers paid most of the taxes while the wealthy paid next to nothing in taxes.

Populists also wanted a more important role in the political process. They wanted to amend the Constitution so that United States senators would be elected by the people. At the time, senators were appointed by the state legislatures. This meant that a big company could "buy" a senator by bribing some legislators. However, not even the biggest company could bribe millions of voters. This proposal would make senators more responsive to the will of the people.

the congressional elections of 1894. The party's candidates did not do very well in those elections. Nevertheless, his efforts to help them made Debs a hero to the Populists. Spending six months in jail made him more of a hero. This was because reporters across the country kept writing about how he had gone to jail for his beliefs.[2]

The Election of 1896

By 1896, many Populists thought that Debs should be their party's nominee for president. At their national convention that year, six state delegations were totally committed to Debs. Sixteen other delegations were mostly in his favor and probably would have voted for him. But at this time, Debs had no personal interest in politics. He was more interested in winning economic justice for the American working class than in winning a political office for himself. He did not travel to the convention in St. Louis to try to win the nomination. Instead, he stayed at home in Terre Haute. He sent a telegram to his chief supporters at the convention asking them to please not nominate him.

During the election of 1896, Debs campaigned for the Populist candidate, William Jennings Bryan. Bryan had also been nominated by the Democrats at their convention that same year. This gave him a good chance of winning the election. In Debs's opinion, Bryan was the best hope for the American working class. Debs believed that Bryan would help the unions in their struggle against the big companies.[3]

Debs was upset when Bryan lost to William McKinley, a pro-business Republican. He was particularly unhappy about the way McKinley won. McKinley carried all of the states in the industrial

East, where working-class people were most numerous. Debs had campaigned tirelessly for Bryan in the East. He believed that the working class would vote for Bryan once they knew that the candidate was a friend of labor.

Debs believed that the working class had been bullied out of voting for Bryan by the big companies. Many companies had formed McKinley Clubs, and the membership dues were given to McKinley's campaign. Workers were given the choice of joining a McKinley Club or getting fired. Other companies told their employees that the factories they worked in would be shut down if Bryan won. Bankers told homeowners who still owed on their homes that their mortgages would be foreclosed if Bryan won. Afraid of losing their jobs and homes, many working-class people in the East voted for McKinley. Many did not vote at all.[4]

For Debs, Bryan's loss was the last straw. The Pullman Strike had shaken his faith that the working class and big companies could work together. The Election of 1896 convinced him that the big companies would not rest until the spirit of the working class was crushed. He gave up his struggle to create unions that could bargain successfully with big companies. Instead, he decided to do something about what he saw as a bigger problem. To Debs, this problem was the American economic system itself—capitalism.[5]

Under capitalism, private individuals own the means of production, like factories, railroads, banks, and farms. Under capitalism, these individuals receive the profits from their businesses. Part of the profits is paid to the employees, the people who do most of the work but do not own any part of the company, as wages. In the nineteenth century, wages were usually, but not always, enough to support a family.

Capitalism encourages companies to compete with one another for the general public's business. It also encourages workers to compete with one another for jobs. Under capitalism, the companies that succeed (and the people who own them) make lots of money. The ones that fail go out of business. Workers with special skills can usually make lots of money. Those with average or no skills often struggle to make ends meet.

To Debs, capitalism meant competition. To him, competition meant that whenever someone wins, someone else has to lose. He believed that as long as big companies dominated the economy, they could also dominate the government. They could do this by bullying the working class out of voting for the candidates of their choice. This is what he believed had happened in the election of 1896. Shortly after the election, on New Year's Day, 1897, Debs became a socialist.[6]

Socialism

Unlike capitalism, socialism makes society the owner of the means of production. This means that the employees receive a greater share of the profits that the companies make. Sometimes, this share is paid in wages, but usually it comes in the form of free public services. These services include such things as a free college education, free public housing, and free health care.

Socialism usually does not involve competition. Instead, the society, represented by the government, decides what the companies it controls will produce and how much they will produce. Workers with special skills do not make as much under socialism as they do under capitalism. However, everyone is guaranteed a job and a decent standard of living.

Socialism can take a number of different forms. In some cases, like in Great Britain, the only means of production the government owns are the utilities, railroads, and shipping docks. In other cases, like in France, the government also owns the largest factories, like the ones that make automobiles or airplanes.

Communism is an extreme version of socialism. Under communism, the government owns everything other than personal property. Everyone, including factory workers and farmers, works for the government. Most people live in government-owned buildings and shop in government-owned stores. Workers are generally free to choose their profession, and skilled workers make more than unskilled ones. The difference in their wages, however, is not as great as under capitalism.

Socialism began in the early 1800s in western Europe. It was a reaction to the Industrial Revolution, when many people left the farms to work in factories. The earliest factories were dark, dirty, and dangerous places to work. Employees had to work twelve to fourteen hours a day, six days a week, just to make enough to get by. Meanwhile, the factory owners were becoming incredibly wealthy. By 1850, many Europeans, particularly in England and Germany, had become disgusted with the way capitalism exploited workers. They developed socialism as a way for everyone to share in the profits produced by industry.

One of the most important of these early socialists was Karl Marx. Marx was born in Germany, but he lived much of his life in England. In England, he saw for himself the harmful effects of the Industrial Revolution on the working class. He wrote *Das Kapital (Capital)* and, with Friedrich Engels, *The Communist Manifesto*. These books explain why

Marx thought socialism was less harmful than capitalism. Marx's books are sometimes difficult to understand, so other socialists wrote simpler versions of what Marx had to say. They also wrote about their own theories of socialism, which were based on Marx's ideas.

The socialists who influenced Debs the most were two Americans, Edward Bellamy and Laurence Gronlund. Bellamy wrote *Looking Backward,* a novel that describes what he thought socialism in America might look like one day. Gronlund wrote *The Cooperative Commonwealth,* which explains his reasons for believing that socialism would someday replace capitalism in the United States.

In a way, Populists were socialists, too. They wanted the federal government to take over the railroads and banks, then distribute the profits to the people in the form of lower shipping rates and lower interest rates on loans.

Debs the Socialist

Debs had experimented with socialism before the election of 1896. In 1895, he became interested in the International Bureau of Correspondence and Agitation. This organization called for "collective ownership of the means of production and distribution." In 1896, he gave his support to the Brotherhood of the Co-operative Commonwealth.

Edward Bellamy was one of Debs's biggest influences. Bellamy was born in Chicopee, Massachusetts, in 1850. His socialist novel Looking Backward (1888) was very popular and inspired over 150 clubs that tried to spread his ideas.

This group wanted to establish a large socialist colony in one of the western states. Debs thought this colony could provide jobs and homes to ARU members who had been blacklisted because of the Pullman Strike.[7]

The death of the ARU was the birth of Debs as a socialist. When the ARU changed its name to the Social Democracy of America (SDA) in 1897, it pledged to help the Brotherhood of the Co-operative Commonwealth establish a western socialist colony. It also pledged to support two of the basic ideas of socialism: public ownership of monopolies and utilities, and public works projects for the unemployed. The ARU's newsletter, *Railway Times*, was renamed *Social Democrat*. Debs became chairman of the SDA.

For the next year Debs toured the country, lecturing about socialism and raising money for the Brotherhood's colony.[8] He was well received by groups eager to hear him speak, but he raised less than three thousand dollars for the colony. By 1898, when the SDA held its second convention, it was clear that there was not enough money to start the colony. At this point, a number of delegates decided to leave the SDA. They formed a political party dedicated to socialism. The splinter group named itself the Social Democratic Party (SDP).

Debs was not one of the leaders of the splinter group, but he soon joined it. For him, the most important thing now was to defeat the companies that kept the working class from enjoying the full fruits of their labor. To him, that meant replacing capitalism with socialism. In late 1898, he accepted a place on the SDP's executive committee. Then, he set out to establish socialism in America.[9]

6

DEBS RUNS FOR PRESIDENT

In some respects, Debs was an odd leader for American socialists. He had never enjoyed school because of all the reading, and the books that most socialist thinkers wrote did not appeal to him. As a thinker and theorist, Debs was held in low regard by Victor Berger and Daniel DeLeon. Berger was the leader of the socialists in Milwaukee, Wisconsin, where he also published a German-language newspaper. DeLeon was the head of the Socialist Labor Party, the first socialist party in America. Both men were appalled by how little Debs knew or cared about socialist theory.

Debs and Socialist Theory

Debs disagreed with the class approach, which Berger supported. This theory held that the working class and the upper class were natural enemies. Debs had nothing against wealthy people. He disliked big companies. He thought that working-class people should lead the attack against the big companies because they had the most to gain from a socialist victory. But he also believed that the working class could unite with the rich to replace capitalism with socialism. This, he believed, would make things better for everyone.

Debs also disagreed with the trade union approach, which DeLeon supported. This theory held that socialists had to take over the unions before they could convert the general population to socialism. Debs believed that working-class people should band together in unions to protect themselves from the big companies. However, he had tried and failed to reform capitalism through his participation in unions. Also, the unions of the day refused to accept African Americans, women, and unskilled workers as members. If capitalism were to be defeated, Debs was sure it would take the efforts of all working-class people, not just a small part of them.

In some respects, Debs was the perfect person to lead American socialists. Berger and DeLeon were not well known except to socialists. They were too rigid in their thinking to appeal to the average American. Their speeches and writings sounded like the work of college professors, not working men. Debs, on the other hand, was known and admired by millions of Americans, even those who did not agree with him. Unlike Berger and DeLeon, Debs had charisma. He was tall, good-looking, and had a tremendous speaking voice, and people understood him. They also sensed that he truly cared for them.

Debs had spent more time than Berger or DeLeon earning his living as a blue-collar worker. This gave him a better understanding of the situation of the working class. He had devoted most of his adult life to helping working-class people get ahead. To prove his devotion to their cause, he had even gone to jail. Neither Berger, who was born in Germany, nor DeLeon, who was born in the West Indies, could legally run for president since they had not been born in the United States. Debs, who was born in Indiana, could.

Most importantly, Debs's version of socialism appealed to more Americans than the versions of Berger and DeLeon. Debs approached socialism from an American point of view, not a Marxist one. He did not think that the working class should destroy the owning class. He believed that all Americans—rich, poor, and in-between—should

Victor Berger believed in a version of socialism that was more strict than Debs's American socialist ideas. When he was twenty, Berger immigrated to Milwaukee from Austria. In 1911, he became the first socialist to be elected to the United States Congress.

work together for the betterment of all. He believed that socialism upheld such traditional American values as helping one's neighbors and working together as a community. He also believed that socialism upheld these values better than capitalism did. He felt this way because socialism promotes cooperation instead of competition.

Debs was concerned that big companies were becoming too powerful. The election of 1896 had taught him that big companies not only dominated the economy, but they threatened to dominate the electoral process as well. If the big companies could tell their employees who to vote for, then many Americans were in danger of losing their rights to liberty and the pursuit of happiness, promised in the Declaration of Independence in 1776. Debs believed it was time to rebel against the tyranny of the big companies, just as the patriots had rebelled against the British over a century before during the American Revolution. In 1776, the patriots had declared their independence from Great Britain. They did this because they wanted to be governed by their own colonial assemblies, not by a King and Parliament who cared little about Americans.

In a way, Debs had become a socialist for the same reasons the signers of the Declaration of Independence had become patriots. To him, a strike was just a modern version of the Boston Tea Party, when colonists had thrown tea into the Boston Harbor to protest an unfair tax. The spirit of the American Revolution, he believed, was all about thirteen colonies helping each other achieve a common goal. By putting the good of the union above the good of any individual state, the patriots had beaten the British. To Debs, socialism attempted to recapture the spirit of 1776 and use it to remake the nation. Just like the American Revolution, American socialism intended to benefit every class, not just the working class. When he presented socialism in this way, Americans understood what he was talking about.[1]

Debs Gets Out the Vote

Debs did not run for office during the congressional election of 1898. Instead, he campaigned for Social Democratic candidates. He spent a lot of time in Fall River and Haverhill, Massachusetts, where textile mill workers were striking. The Social Democrats only received twelve thousand votes in the entire country in 1898. A majority of them were in Massachusetts, where Debs had campaigned.[2] Two socialists were elected to the Massachusetts state legislature and another was elected mayor of Haverhill. Their victories made Debs a hero of the party. He became more of a hero in 1899, when he recruited a large number of new members while on a speaking tour in Texas.

In 1900, the Social Democrats met in Indianapolis for their first national convention. Debs was their leading candidate for president, and it seemed certain that he would win the nomination. But he was still not thinking in terms of a political career for himself. He had said publicly just a few months earlier that he had no intention of running for public office. Right after his name was placed in nomination, he asked the convention to nominate someone else.

All that night Debs was hounded to change his mind. The party was torn by factions, each pushing its own theory of socialism. The representatives of each faction insisted that only Debs had the charisma and the popularity to unite the party. They insisted that only he could lead it to victory in the election of 1900. Eventually, he let himself be convinced. Renominated the next day, he accepted while the delegates cheered.[3]

The Election of 1900

Debs did not succeed in uniting the Social Democrats, but he did get them to work together during the election of 1900. He toured the country for the party's candidates, and he spoke about socialism in a way that got people's attention. He campaigned so hard he even scared the two major parties. The Democrats charged that he was being secretly financed by the Republicans. The Republicans charged that he planned to drop out in favor of William Jennings Bryan, the Democratic candidate.

After the votes were counted, the Social Democrats were not surprised by the outcome. Debs had lost to the Republican candidate, William McKinley. They were surprised, however, to discover that Debs had received almost one hundred thousands votes. This was far more than any socialist candidate had ever received for president of the United States.[4]

Once the election was over, the socialist factions started squabbling among themselves again. This never made sense to Debs. He was not a rigid thinker like many socialists. He believed that socialism was not about learning fancy theories. Instead, it was about understanding that big companies must give a fair share of their profits to the working class. It made little difference to him which faction had the more "correct" understanding of socialist theory. To Debs, socialists were all in the same boat. Instead of arguing with each other, they should work together to replace capitalism.[5]

The Socialist Party of America

In July 1901, most of the factions came together at a socialist convention in Indianapolis. Except for a few members of DeLeon's Socialist Labor Party, they formed the Socialist Party of America (SPA). Then they agreed to work together for the same immediate goals. Debs hated the kind of political squabbling that went on at conventions, and he did not attend this one. He excused himself by claiming that someone in his family was sick. Despite his non-attendance, he remained the unofficial leader of the SPA.[6]

Between the convention in 1901 and the congressional elections of 1902, Debs gave a national lecture tour on behalf of the SPA. Protestant ministers, small businesspeople, and working-class men and women all found something in his message to cheer them. He worked especially hard to spread socialism in the ranks of the working class by getting involved once again in unionism.

In 1902, the largest labor organization in the United States was the American Federation of Labor (AFL). The AFL had been founded in 1886 to unite workers of all trades. In order to survive after the Panic of 1893, the AFL had been forced to become a partner with the big companies. It promised not to strike and not to recruit African Americans, women, and unskilled workers. In return, the big companies paid AFL members higher wages than non-AFL members received. Because it excluded so many people from membership, the AFL was not strong enough to challenge the big companies. This, of course, was exactly what the big companies wanted. Although the AFL survived, it was unable to do much for the working class in general.

The American Labor Union

In 1902, Debs helped to do something about this situation. That same year, the Western Labor Union (WLU) voted to make itself into a national union. As the Western Federation of Miners, the WLU had withdrawn from the AFL in 1897. It did so because it did not approve of the AFL's partnership with big companies. By 1902, western miners realized that belonging to a national labor organization might get them a better deal from the big companies. However, they wanted a national union that would be more independent of the big companies than the AFL.

Debs helped reorganize the WLU into the American Labor Union (ALU). He also helped introduce it into AFL territory, the industrial East. The ALU constitution allowed any worker, regardless of trade or skill level, to join. Debs's involvement with the ALU gave it instant respectability. Many of its members also joined the SPA.[7]

Many SPA members were angry about Debs's role in forming the ALU. For years, socialists who believed in the trade union approach had been rising up through the ranks of the AFL. They thought they were on the verge of taking it over. Now, the ALU was threatening to become a larger and more important union since it was open to all working-class people. What these socialists failed to understand was that they could never take over the AFL as long as it remained partners with the big companies. Samuel Gompers, president of the AFL, made this clear at the AFL's convention in 1903.[8]

Debs did not care that some socialists were angry about the ALU. He was convinced that the AFL was never going to do anything in the fight against capitalism anyway. Better, he thought, to help create a radical new labor organization that would. To this end, in 1905 he helped the ALU reorganize itself into the Industrial Workers of the World (IWW). Unlike the AFL, the IWW offered membership to anyone who worked for wages. The IWW did not care about anyone's trade, skill, race, gender, or national origin. It criticized the AFL's partnership with the big companies. Most importantly, it vowed to be a strong voice for the rights of working-class people, especially the right to strike.[9]

The SPA made some impressive gains in the state and local elections of 1902. No socialists were elected to Congress, but several became mayors and state legislators. Also, the overall vote total for socialists was about double what it had been in 1900. At its national convention in 1904, it had more than twenty-three thousand dues-paying members, a big increase from less than five thousand in 1900.[10]

The Election of 1904

Once again the convention nominated Debs for president. Once again he tried to refuse the nomination. Once again he was talked into accepting it by the party's leadership. Once again he ran hard, criss-crossing the nation during several campaign tours. And once again he lost, this time to the Republican candidate, Theodore Roosevelt. But this time Debs polled more than four hundred thousand votes, more than four times his vote total in 1900. This impressive showing proved that the Socialists were getting out their message to the American people. The huge increase in the socialist vote suggested that the SPA might do even better in elections to come.[11]

Then came the congressional election of 1906. The SPA did not do as well as it had expected. The vote total for all SPA candidates was down from more than four hundred thousand votes in 1904 to less than three hundred thousand. Many socialists blamed this decline on the rise of progressivism. In 1906, progressivism was sweeping the United States, and it had taken root in both of the major parties.[12]

Progressivism

Progressivism was a social reform movement that began in the 1880s. The movement started as an effort to help disadvantaged immigrants adjust to life in urban, industrial America. By 1900, Progressives were working to get rid of corruption in politics and government. They were also working to curb the growing economic power of the big companies.

Progressivism was a lot like populism. Several of the Populist proposals, such as an income tax and the direct election of senators, were made into law by the Progressives. Progressives were also responsible for reforming public education, winning women the right to vote, and prohibiting the sale of alcohol.

Progressives came from every class, occupation, and geographical region. They were most influential during the 1910s, when they successfully amended the Constitution four times. Progressivism faded away after 1924. It had died out by the time of the Great Depression in the 1930s.

The Election of 1908

By the election of 1908, Debs had put the IWW behind him and was ready to move on. The SPA was ready to move on, too. With forty-one thousand dues-paying members and more than three thousand local chapters, the party thought it might poll a million votes.[13] At its convention in Chicago, Debs was nominated for president almost unanimously. This time he did not have to be begged to run. However, he still had no desire to actually be president of the United States. He ran because he saw the election as the perfect vehicle for educating the American public about socialism.

To get out the vote in a major way, the SPA made use of the encampment and the Red Special. The encampment was intended to attract farmers in the Southwest. It appealed especially to those who rented small holdings in isolated areas from one year to the next. The idea was borrowed from the Populists, who had used it in the 1880s and 1890s. Thousands of farm families were invited to week-long gatherings where they could feast, dance, and learn about socialism. Farmers came in their horse-drawn wagons from as far as one hundred miles away. Debs was the main attraction, and at just about every encampment he lectured about socialism for hours on end to an enthusiastic audience.[14]

The Red Special—red is the color of socialism— was a train that the SPA had hired. It consisted of a locomotive, a sleeping car, and a baggage car. The train carried Debs, a brass band, and reams of campaign literature across America. Leaving Chicago in late August, the Red Special set out on a four-week tour of the West. The idea was for Debs to speak before a large audience each night in a major city. Along the way, he would speak to smaller crowds at a dozen or so stops each day. When the Red Special pulled back into Chicago at the end of the tour, Debs had traveled nine thousand miles and spoken to two hundred seventy-five thousand people in almost two hundred cities and towns.[15]

The Red Special was a homecoming as well as a campaign tour. At just about every stop, at least one of Debs's old comrades in the American Railway Union came to greet him. He almost always remembered them, and they delighted the crowds by reliving old memories of the Pullman Strike.

After a brief rest, Debs and the Red Special headed east. The results were much the same as in the West. In New York City, Debs rode through the working-class residential district on the back of a flatbed truck. So many people came to hear him that the truck stopped every few blocks so everyone could hear Debs deliver his speech. The tour ended

The Red Special, with Debs's photo on the front, is seen here.

on Election Day with a parade of fourteen thousand workingmen through the streets of Chicago.[16]

The encampments and the Red Special generated lots of excitement. Debs and his fellow socialists eagerly awaited the election returns. No one actually expected Debs to win, but they all hoped for a million or more votes. They were quite disappointed. The final tally for Debs showed slightly more than four hundred and twenty thousand. This was an increase of less than twenty thousand votes over the number he had polled four years earlier.[17]

Debs was not greatly disappointed by the results of the election of 1908. Better than anyone, he knew that he had never been a serious contender for the presidency. In a way, he must have been relieved. He always said it was an office he did not really want. Instead, he was thankful that there were four hundred thousand committed socialists in the United States.[18]

Life on the Road

Running for president was hard on Debs. He continued to do it because he loved to travel. At home in Terre Haute, Debs was a member in good standing of the middle class. As a former city clerk and state legislator, he was a respected member of the community. Owning a publishing company made him a businessman, even though it never made him very much money. His style of dress marked him as respectable middle class, too. He almost always appeared in public wearing a white shirt, suit, and necktie.

In his heart, however, Debs was a workingman. This is one reason why he continued to belong to the Brotherhood of Locomotive Firemen long after he had stopped being a fireman. Life on the road meant that he got to associate with working-class people all across the country and join in their boisterous good times.

As a presidential candidate, Debs no longer had to ride in locomotive cabs or empty boxcars. However, the SPA lacked the funds for him to travel first-class, so he cut corners wherever he could. He rarely stayed in a sleeping car. Instead, he usually slept, sitting straight up, on a bench seat in a coach car. He spent the night with working-class people whenever he could. Sometimes they could offer him nothing better than a pillow and a blanket on the floor. Otherwise he stayed in cheap hotels, which were usually old and rundown.

A typical Debs campaign stop was a whirlwind affair. He gave one or more speeches, any one of which could go on for two hours. Then, it was time to socialize with his fellow workers. Usually, this meant drinking in one or more saloons. In the early hours of the morning, Debs would return to wherever he was staying. Instead of sleeping, though, he usually stayed up until dawn talking strategy with local socialists. He rarely ate a decent meal. Instead, he grabbed a bite to eat whenever he could.

On the road, Debs drank too much, smoked too much, and swore too much. He told dirty jokes and he never went to church. It was the kind of life he loved. However, one reason for the decline of his health was the way he lived while he was on the road.[19]

Theodore and Kate

Unlike modern presidential candidates, Debs did not have a large staff. Usually, he traveled alone. He relied on local socialists to help him when he arrived in their community. However, he did have the services of his younger brother, Theodore Debs, who was also a devoted socialist.

Theodore was Debs's right-hand man. When Debs went on the road, Theodore answered his mail, managed his finances, and got his articles ready for the printer. Sometimes, Theodore would go to a city or town ahead of Debs, just to get things ready for his next speech. When Debs needed something on the road, Theodore sent it to him. When Debs needed advice, or just someone to talk to about the difficulties of what he was trying to do, he usually

Eugene V. Debs (right) is greeted by his brother, Theodore.

talked to Theodore. When their parents, who were getting old, needed looking after, it was Theodore, not Debs, who took care of them. Theodore even turned down a good-paying job with a Terre Haute bank just so he could work as his older brother's personal secretary.

Debs relied heavily on Theodore's support. He paid him a salary from the money he received for writing articles and giving speeches. He remarked many times that Theodore was a great source of strength for him. Without Theodore's help, Debs probably could not have traveled the way he did.[20]

Theodore did not get along very well with Debs's wife, Kate. Kate loved her husband, but she did not share his ideas about socialism. She would have been much happier if Debs had stopped his traveling and taken a job in Terre Haute. She sometimes did not see Debs for weeks at a time, and when he returned from a tour he was usually sick and tired. It was then her duty to nurse him back to health. Once he was feeling better, he was up and on his way, leaving her alone again.

Kate Debs resented her situation. She seems to have taken out some of her frustration on Theodore. She seemed to feel that her brother-in-law helped keep her husband on the road and away from her. She also did not like that Debs gave Theodore anywhere from one third to one half of his earnings from speaking and writing. She did not appreciate how much Theodore did for Debs. Instead, she thought of Theodore as a sponge who took money from her husband without doing anything in return.[21]

Debs knew that the two most important people in his life did not like each other, but he did little about it. He loved his wife, even though he spent much of his time away from home. He loved his brother, too, and he needed Theodore to help him accomplish his goals. He seems to have dealt with their dislike for one another by laughing it off when he could and ignoring it when he could not.[22]

Debs Takes a Break

Debs was exhausted by all the campaigning he had done in 1908. For the first time in his life, he took off several months to recuperate. He wrote several articles a week for the *Appeal to Reason*, a socialist newspaper. Other than that, he mostly just lounged around the house. Giving a dozen or more speeches each day had worn out his throat. He went to see several doctors, but they just told him to rest up and take it easy. He did have his throat operated on in 1910, but no one seems to know exactly what was wrong with it. Whatever was wrong, the operation did not fix his throat.[23]

The election of 1908 disappointed socialists, but the party continued to grow. By 1910, the number of SPA members had almost doubled to about eighty thousand. Even better, the congressional, state, and local elections of 1910 and 1911 gave socialists many things to cheer about. Nationwide, the party's candidates polled almost seven hundred thousand votes. Almost ninety socialists got elected to state and local offices. Twenty of them were voted into their state legislatures. In Wisconsin, socialist Victor Berger got elected to the U. S. House of Representatives.[24]

The Election of 1912

The SPA went into the election of 1912 with high hopes. Party membership stood at one hundred eighteen thousand, and this time the forces of progressivism were seriously split.[25] The Republicans re-nominated President William Taft and the Democrats nominated Woodrow Wilson. After failing to win the Republican nomination, former president Theodore Roosevelt left the party to join the Progressive, or Bull Moose, Party. All three presidential candidates were Progressives. Meanwhile, the SPA had again nominated Debs for president. Socialists hoped that a three-way split among Progressive voters would make it easier for Debs to win.

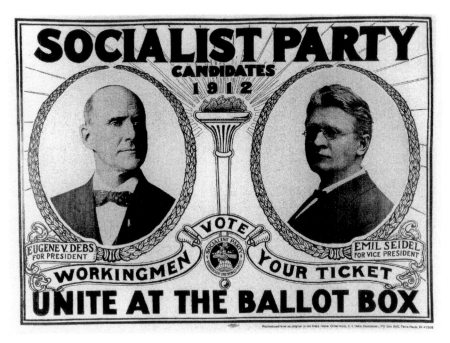

This 1912 campaign poster features Eugene V. Debs and his running mate Emil Seidel. If Debs had been elected president, Seidel would have served as his vice president.

As always, Debs ran an energetic campaign. He delivered a dozen or more speeches almost every day from late June until Election Day. This time, neither he nor the SPA were disappointed with the results. Wilson won the election, but Debs polled more than nine hundred thousand votes. This was over double the number he had received in 1908. Eight more cities elected socialists to a major office, and twenty more socialists got elected to their state legislatures.[26]

The election of 1912 was the high point for the SPA. Debs polled more votes for president than ever before. SPA candidates for state and local offices had demonstrated that they had a reasonable chance of winning. In the days shortly after the election, all things seemed possible for the Socialists.

7

DEBS GOES TO PRISON

Debs returned to his home in Terre Haute after the 1912 campaign to rest and recuperate. He had just turned fifty-seven. For the last twenty years or so he had abused his body by traveling in drafty railcars, staying in cheap hotel rooms, staying up all night, drinking too much, and not eating properly. Now this lifestyle was catching up with him.

For the next nine months, Debs rarely left his house. He spent much of his time in bed. Instead of getting better, he seemed to get worse. In September 1913, he suffered a physical and emotional breakdown. His family sent him to a sanitarium in Estes Park, Colorado, to recover. Six weeks worth of fresh mountain air, wholesome food, strenuous physical activity, and pleasant companions revitalized him. By Christmas he was back in Terre Haute.

Debs Tries Semi-Retirement

The breakdown scared Debs. For the first time he began thinking about retiring. His views were highly thought of in the socialist community. He could easily make a living writing articles for pro-socialist newspapers. In early 1914, he made plans to do exactly that. He resigned from the *Appeal to Reason*, cancelled plans for a national speaking tour, and began to take life easy.

After a few months of inactivity, Debs began feeling restless. His health was slowly returning, and he was eager to get out on the road again. In 1914, Frank O'Hare, editor of the *National Rip-Saw*, a socialist newspaper in St. Louis, Missouri, contacted him. O'Hare offered Debs a position as an editorial writer and lecturer. Debs quickly accepted.[1]

World War I

By the end of the year, Debs had something to write and speak about other than American socialism. In August 1914, World War I broke out in Europe. All across the continent, socialists began putting aside their differences with capitalists to unite against the enemies of their nations. This behavior appalled

Debs. He knew that the people most likely to be killed during the war were working-class people serving as common soldiers and sailors. He began writing and speaking about how necessary it was for socialists to refuse to take part in this war.

To Debs's mind, World War I had been caused by capitalist competition between the major trading nations of Europe. He believed that capitalists were fighting the war to achieve two goals. One was to destroy their trading rivals in other countries. The other was to crush their socialist rivals within their own countries. The working class was being recruited to its own destruction by capitalist appeals to patriotism. Regardless of which side won, Debs believed that World War I was going to weaken the working class and destroy the socialist movement.

Debs's health kept him from doing everything he wanted to do as an anti-war activist. In 1915, he suffered another major breakdown. Once again he went away for six weeks to a sanitarium. Although he did recover somewhat, a year later he still was not feeling well. When the SPA tried to nominate him for president in 1916, he refused. In his place, the party nominated Allan L. Benson, a journalist.

Debs did allow himself to be nominated by the SPA of Terre Haute to run for Congress. He campaigned with as much energy as he could muster. He drove to every village in the district and gave speeches in town squares to anyone who would listen. But the election of 1916 was not a good one for the SPA or for Debs. Benson polled only two-thirds as many votes as Debs had in 1912. Debs himself lost by a large margin to his Republican opponent.[2]

Mabel Curry

During his campaign for Congress, Debs came to know Mabel Dunlap Curry. She had lived just a few blocks from his house for years. He was rarely ever home, though, so he never got to know her until 1916. Curry was an educated, intelligent woman. She was also friendly and outgoing. Like Debs, she wrote articles for national newspapers. She also gave speaking tours, talking mostly about why women should have the right to vote.

Debs and Curry fell in love with each other. Nothing ever happened, though. Both had been married to someone else for a long time, and they did not want to hurt their spouses' feelings. Also, Debs felt obligated to his wife, Kate. For years, she had given him the freedom to travel about the country without requiring very much from him in return. She had also nursed him back to health whenever he had returned from a road trip. Whether or not Debs still loved Kate, and he probably did, he felt he owed her a tremendous debt. Leaving her for another woman was not the way to repay it. Debs and

Curry's schedules kept them on the move, so they did not have time for a traditional romance. Every now and then they were able to meet, usually at Theodore Debs's house. But mostly their relationship was restricted to writing letters to each other.[3]

Debs Attacks World War I

In 1917, Debs suffered a third physical breakdown. Once again he had to go to a sanitarium to recuperate. Then, in April 1917, the United States declared war on Germany, thus entering World War I.

Debs continued to write articles and editorials urging his fellow socialists to oppose the war. He was mostly ignored. Many American socialists made every effort to show their total support for American involvement in the war. Some socialist journals that had eagerly published Debs's articles in the past now refused to accept them. Although they applauded his socialist ideas, they did not like his antiwar views.

Another problem for Debs was the passage of the Espionage Act in 1917. This act gave the federal government the power to imprison anyone who spoke out against the American war effort. Several of his socialist friends were arrested and jailed. Their crime was urging American citizens to refuse to participate in the war. Because of his poor health,

Though many people argued that the Espionage Act infringed on Americans' right to free speech, President Woodrow Wilson considered anyone who violated the act a traitor to the nation.

Debs could do little more for his fellow socialists than cheer them on from the sidelines.[4]

By the spring of 1918, Debs could not sit and watch things happen any more. The success of the Bolshevik Revolution in Russia the year before encouraged him greatly. However, it also depressed him when he thought of how far the United States was from a socialist revolution. Other things depressed him, as well. Many of his friends were in jail. He could get little of his work published. Socialists were arguing with each other about supporting the war effort. The federal government had begun to persecute the SPA because some of its members opposed the war. Although his health still was not good, Debs made up his mind to take action.

Debs Gets Arrested

Debs pulled himself out of bed at the end of May. He forced himself to spend the next two weeks giving antiwar speeches across Indiana and Illinois. These failed to attract the attention of the authorities, so he decided to speak at the convention of the Ohio Socialist Party in mid-June in Canton. There, he would give a speech that he hoped would lead to his arrest.[5]

When the federal government locked up unknown agitators, the media and the general public paid no attention. But Debs was a nationally known figure who was admired by more people than had voted for him in the past. If someone like Debs could get arrested and locked up for protesting the war, it would get plenty of media attention. He hoped it would be enough to end American involvement in the war and the persecution of his socialist comrades.[6]

On June 16, 1918, Debs gave his famous speech at Nimisilla Park in Canton, Ohio. He was arrested two weeks later for violating the Espionage Act. He was released on bail after spending the night in jail. For the next several months, he made a series of speeches in favor of SPA candidates and causes.

Debs on Trial

Debs's trial began on September 9, 1918, in Cleveland, Ohio. For two days, the prosecution paraded one witness after another. All of them said that Debs had spoken against the war in the presence of draft-age men. This was a violation of the Espionage Act. When it came time for Debs's attorneys to present their case, there was not much they could do. Debs cheerfully admitted that the government's witnesses had told the truth. When given the chance to say what he wanted, he gave a rousing, two-hour speech in court about the inevitable triumph of socialism. The only defense he offered was that the Espionage Act itself was unconstitutional.

He claimed this because he believed the act violated his First Amendment right to freedom of speech. But this was not a matter for the federal district court to decide. The judge, David C. Westenhaver, found Debs guilty and sentenced him to ten years in prison.

Debs's attorneys announced that they would appeal the conviction to the Supreme Court. Westenhaver allowed Debs to go free until the Supreme Court made its decision. However, he made Debs promise to stay either in Terre Haute or Cleveland. Over the next six months, Debs gave several speeches in those cities and wrote a few articles for the socialist press. On March 10, 1919, the Supreme Court upheld Westenhaver's decision by a vote of 9–0. On April 13, Debs was sent to prison.[7]

Debs in Prison

The state of West Virginia had a contract with the federal government to house federal prisoners in the West Virginia State Penitentiary in Moundsville. This is where Debs was sent. The warden of the prison, Joseph Z. Terrell, treated him as if he were an honored guest. Terrell let Debs have as many visitors and write as many letters as he liked. Debs was also free to roam about the penitentiary as he pleased.

The inmates were delighted to have Debs among them. For one thing, Debs always treated them with

While Debs was in prison, petitions were signed in order to try to get him set free. This booth in his hometown of Terre Haute collected over twenty-one thousand signatures.

respect. For another, his efforts to make life better for the working class convinced the inmates that he held their best interests at heart. For the next two months, Debs listened to the problems of the inmates. He also read and wrote letters for those who were illiterate.

After two months, space became available in the federal prison in Atlanta, Georgia, and Debs was transferred there. Debs's new warden, Fred G. Zerbst, was only slightly tougher on him than Terrell had been. Zerbst restricted Debs's mail and visiting privileges. But he offered Debs an easy job in the hospital and extended him more privileges than the average prisoner received.

Debs became a favorite of the inmates in Atlanta, just as he had been in Moundsville. His presence in the prison seemed to bring about better conditions for all the prisoners. However, the hot Georgia summer and the poor food took their toll

Debs on the Management of Prisons

Debs was fairly well-treated in prison, but he could see that his fellow inmates often were not. To Debs, prison should be a place where criminals are rehabilitated. He believed this could best be done by treating prisoners with kindness and respect. Instead, prisoners were treated callously, sometimes even cruelly. Their rights and privileges were restricted. They were expected to follow the rules without question. Rather than being treated like adults, prisoners were usually treated like children or animals.

Such treatment moved Debs to write:

I marvel at the incredible stupidity that blinds men in control of prisons to the redeeming power of kindness as a substitute for the destructive power of brutality. Every instinct of our nature protests against cruelty to the helpless and defenseless, yet of all places where it is most needed mercy is least practiced in the treatment of convicts.[8]

on Debs's health. Many feared that he would die in prison.[9]

Debs Runs for President from Prison

Debs never fully recovered from his confinement in prison. Indeed, he had not been in the best of health when he went in. But by 1920, while still in prison, he had recovered enough that the SPA once again nominated him for president.

The move made sense for several reasons. First, Debs was the best-known socialist in the country, and he was a proven vote-getter. Second, many Americans were dismayed that such a man as Debs could be locked up simply for speaking his mind. The party hoped to capture some of their outrage on election day. Also, the party was falling apart. In August of 1919, two splinter groups broke away from the SPA. They formed the Communist Party and the Communist Labor Party. The remaining members of the SPA hoped that Debs's candidacy could somehow restore the unity of the American socialist movement. This was because Debs was the only person admired by all three factions.

The Election of 1920

Obviously, Debs could not campaign as he had in the past. Zerbst did let him give one press conference per week. He also allowed Debs more

These buttons are still sold today through the Eugene V. Debs Foundation.

visiting and letter-writing privileges than before. Meanwhile, the SPA made the most of Debs's imprisonment. They adopted "From the Prison to the White House" as their campaign slogan. They made up campaign buttons featuring a photograph of Debs wearing prison garb and standing in front of bars. Around the edge of the button, printed in white letters on a red background, was the slogan, "For President— Convict No. 9653." Surprisingly, the election of 1920 was Debs's best showing ever. He received more than 919,000 votes for president, slightly more than he had polled in 1912.[10]

Debs did not come close to winning the election, having polled only about 6 percent of the vote. His showing, however, made many Americans think about his imprisonment. It also made them think about the other federal prisoners who had spoken out against the war. In 1921, a campaign to win him a presidential pardon sprang up. Hundreds of thousands of Americans signed petitions to get

Eugene V. Debs, in his prisoner's uniform, shakes hands with his running mate, Seymour Stedman, at Atlanta Federal Penitentiary in 1920.

Debs out of jail. President Woodrow Wilson refused to grant Debs a pardon because he thought Debs was a traitor. Also, Debs had insulted Wilson in his anti-war speeches.

Wilson's successor, Warren G. Harding, saw things a little differently. Debs had not insulted Harding during the war as he had Wilson. Also, the ratification of the peace treaty between the United States and Germany in November of 1921 officially ended the war. This made it easier for Harding to grant Debs a pardon. On December 23, 1921, Harding announced that Debs and twenty-three other prisoners who had opposed the war would be pardoned on Christmas Day. Harding even invited Debs to visit him in the White House on his way home to Terre Haute, which Debs did.[11]

Thirty months in prison just about destroyed Debs's health. His stomach and kidneys bothered him. He had a headache almost constantly. He suffered from rheumatism and lower back pain. He was in such bad shape that he had to make several lengthy visits to Lindlahr Sanitarium in Elmhurst, Illinois, during his remaining years.

Nevertheless, Debs found the strength to remain active in SPA affairs. He condemned the three factions that had arisen while he was in prison, and he tried to get them to agree on basic socialist ideals. He made a few more speeches, wrote a few more articles, and even served one last time as the SPA's chairman.

In 1926, Debs and his wife Kate went to Bermuda for five weeks. It was the first vacation they had taken since their honeymoon more than forty years earlier. After returning to Terre Haute, Debs's health problems flared up once again. He returned to Lindlahr Sanitarium, where he died on October 20, 1926, at the age of seventy.[12]

A passionate speaker, Eugene V. Debs had a profound effect on the America of his time. Here, he speaks in Milwaukee, Wisconsin, in the summer of 1924, only two years before his death.

8

DEBS: FAILURE OR SUCCESS?

In some respects, Eugene Debs was a big failure. He co-founded three organizations—the American Railway Union, the Industrial Workers of the World, and the Socialist Party of America—but none of them achieved much success while he was alive. The ARU died during his lifetime and the IWW died shortly afterwards. The SPA survived for years, but it never did much of anything. Debs ran for president five times and never came close to winning. He spent three years in prison. He never made much money, he neglected his health, and he died prematurely. Eugene Debs is a strange model for an American success story.

Debs the Failure

As leader of the SPA, Debs was too weak to overcome the factional disputes that plagued the party during his lifetime. He saw correctly that the United States was a class society. He also saw that the gap between the haves and the have-nots, the owning class and the working class, was growing wider every day. At the same time, he failed to realize that most Americans had tremendous faith that American democracy could close that gap.

Most Americans continued to believe that "all men are created equal." They also believed that hard work and perseverance could lift workingmen out of the working class. They believed this because they saw it happening all around them. It did not happen as often as they would have liked. However, it happened often enough to make movement to a higher class a reality for many American workers. In time, the majority of the working class earned enough money to become a permanent part of the middle class.

Like most socialists, Debs failed to recognize just how flexible the American system is. Karl Marx, the great socialist theorist, taught that capitalists would never share their wealth with the working class. He also taught that they could not be made to share, and this would lead to their downfall. The only way to achieve a better deal for the working class was to overthrow capitalism and replace it with socialism. But while socialists were calling for a complete overhaul of the system, the Progressives found a way to change things by working within the system.

By the time of Debs's death in 1925, the Progressives had largely succeeded. Some Progressives created their own political party. Most joined either the Democrats or the Republicans. Eventually, they were able to take over both major parties. Once this happened, Progressives were able to change many things. They imposed an income tax on the wealthy. They made it so that United States senators were elected directly by the people. They won women the right to vote. They prohibited the sale of alcohol. They reformed state and local governments by reducing the power of the wealthy to control politics. Perhaps most importantly from a socialist point of view, they broke up the big companies by outlawing monopolies and other unfair business practices.

Social and economic reform did not end with the Progressives. Between 1925 and 1950, Americans won a number of benefits, including Social Security, minimum wage, a shorter work week and workday, workmen's compensation, industrial safety regulations, welfare programs for the needy, and better public education. All these things benefited the working class far more than the wealthy class.

Debs the Success

By all accounts, Debs was admired and respected by just about everyone who ever met him. He had a reputation for giving away his money, his shirt, his overcoat, even his watch, to strangers who had a greater need for them. Most everyone, even those who disagreed with him, commented about what a great, caring man Debs was. Some people likened him to Abraham Lincoln and Jesus Christ, and many called him a saint.[1]

Debs gave hope to millions of Americans. He traveled among them and shared their lives. He wanted to make them feel good about themselves and their futures. He worked hard to bring about his dream of a better world through socialism, and he did not care too much that most people did not share this dream. It was enough for him that he was able to spread the word of socialism to people who might embrace it someday. Whether they did or not, Debs had done his job. He died secure in the knowledge that he had done everything he could do to make the world a better place to live.

So, in some respects, Debs was a huge success. All his life, he remained true to what he believed in. He spent his years actively working to improve life for his fellow citizens. In the process, he won thousands of friends and millions of admirers. The nation mourned his passing.[2]

GLOSSARY

boycott—When a group of people decide not to buy from or deal with a certain business.

brakeman—The member of a train crew who stops the train.

capitalism—The economic system whereby the means of production are owned by private individuals.

communism—A form of socialism whereby the government owns all the means of production.

conductor—The member of a train crew who decides when and where the train will stop.

engineer—The member of a train crew who drives the locomotive.

fireman—The member of a train crew who keeps the fire burning in the locomotive's steam engine.

injunction—A court order forbidding someone from doing a certain thing.

negotiate—To talk with someone in the hope of working out a deal.

populism—An 1870s movement that tried to reform the American economy and government.

progressivism—A late-nineteenth- early-twentieth-century movement that greatly reformed the American economy and government.

railroad worker—Any worker, other than management, who works for a railroad.

socialism—The economic system whereby the government owns some of the means of production.

strike—When most of a company's workers refuse to work.

switchman—The member of a train crew who switches passenger and freight cars from track to track.

working class—Workers who work with their hands for a living; blue-collar workers and their families.

CHRONOLOGY

1855—Born in Terre Haute, Indiana.

1869—Drops out of school and goes to work for the Vandalia Railroad.

1873—The Panic of 1873 puts thousands of working-class people out of work.

1874—Moves to St. Louis, Missouri; returns to Terre Haute and goes to work for Hulman & Cox.

1875—Joins the Brotherhood of Locomotive Firemen.

1877—The first national railroad strike takes place.

1879—Is elected city clerk of Terre Haute.

1880—Becomes secretary-treasurer of the BLF and editor of the *Locomotive Firemen's Magazine*.

1884—Goes on the road as a BLF recruiter.

1885—Is elected to the Indiana state legislature as a Democrat; Marries Kate Metzel.

1889—The Chicago, Burlington & Quincy strike fails; Debs helps form the Supreme Council of the United Orders of Railway Employees.

1893—Helps form the American Railway Union; The Panic of 1893 puts thousands of working-class people out of work.

1894—The ARU wins the Great Northern Strike but loses the Pullman Strike; Debs is arrested for his role in the Pullman Strike.

1895—Spends six months in the McHenry County, Illinois, jail.

1896—Campaigns for Populist candidates in the election of 1896.

1898—Joins the Social Democratic Party.

1900—Runs for president as a Socialist and receives almost one hundred thousand votes.

1901—Helps form the Socialist Party of America.

1902—Helps form the American Labor Union, later known as the International Workers of the World.

1904—Runs for president and receives more than four hundred thousand votes.

1908—Runs for president and receives more than four hundred twenty thousand votes.

1912—Runs for president and receives more than nine hundred thousand votes.

1914—World War I begins.

1916—Runs for Congress but loses.

1917—The United States enters World War I; Congress passes the Espionage Act.

1918—Is arrested for protesting American involvement in World War I.

1919—Goes to prison to serve a ten-year sentence.

1920—Runs for president from prison and receives more than nine hundred nineteen thousand votes.

1921—Is pardoned by President Warren G. Harding.

1926—Dies in Elmhurst, Illinois.

CHAPTER NOTES

Chapter 1. Debs Makes a Speech

1. Seymour M. Lipset and Gary Marks, *It Didn't Happen Here: Why Socialism Failed in the United States* (New York: W.W. Norton, 2000), p. 282.

2. Ray Ginger, *The Bending Cross: A Biography of Eugene Victor Debs* (New York: Russell & Russell, 1969), pp. 53, 82, 270, 292.

3. Ibid., pp. 354–356.

4. Eugene V. Debs, "Socialism and the Great War: Speech at Canton, Ohio, June 16, 1918," in John Gabriel Hunt, ed., *The Dissenters: America's Voices of Opposition* (New York: Gramercy Books, 1993), pp. 206–222.

5. Hunt, pp. 207–209.

6. Ibid., pp. 211–212.

7. Ibid.

8. Ibid., pp. 206–222.

9. Harold W. Currie, *Eugene V. Debs* (Boston: Twayne Publishers, 1976), p. 89.

10. Ginger, pp. 358–359.

Chapter 2. Working on the Railroad

1. Marguerite Young, *Harp Song for a Radical: The Life and Times of Eugene Victor Debs* (New York: Alfred A. Knopf, 1999), pp. 181–185.

2. Ray Ginger, *The Bending Cross: A Biography of Eugene Victor Debs* (New York: Russell & Russell, 1969), p. 9.

3. Harold W. Currie, *Eugene V. Debs* (Boston: Twayne Publishers, 1976), p. 18.

4. Young, p. 263.

5. Nick Salvatore, *Eugene V. Debs: Citizen and Socialist* (Urbana: University of Illinois Press, 1982), pp. 12, 17.

6. Young, pp. 264–265.

7. Ibid., pp. 267–269.

8. Currie, pp. 18–19.

Chapter 3. The Brotherhood of Locomotive Firemen

1. Harold W. Currie, *Eugene V. Debs* (Boston: Twayne Publishers, 1976), p. 19.

2. Nick Salvatore, *Eugene V. Debs: Citizen and Socialist* (Urbana: University of Illinois Press, 1982), pp. 20–21.

3. Ray Ginger, *The Bending Cross: A Biography of Eugene Victor Debs* (New York: Russell & Russell, 1969), pp. 22–23.

4. Marguerite Young, *Harp Song for a Radical: The Life and Times of Eugene Victor Debs* (New York: Alfred A. Knopf, 1999), pp. 483–495.

5. Ginger, pp. 29–31.

6. Salvatore, p. 27.

7. Ginger, p. 30.

8. Salvatore, pp. 27–29, 48–50.

9. Ginger, pp. 32–33.

10. Ibid., p. 33.

11. Ibid., pp. 39, 40, 69.

12. Young, pp. 319–350.

13. Ginger, p. 61.

14. Ibid., pp. 62, 298, 385.

15. Salvatore, pp. 57–59.

16. Ginger, pp. 38–40, 47, 55.

17. Salvatore, pp. 73–77.

18. Ginger, pp. 58, 64, 66, 73–80.

Chapter 4. The American Railway Union

1. Nick Salvatore, *Eugene V. Debs: Citizen and Socialist* (Urbana: University of Illinois Press, 1982), p. 115.

2. Harold W. Currie, *Eugene V. Debs* (Boston: Twayne Publishers, 1976), pp. 23–24.

3. Ray Ginger, *The Bending Cross: A Biography of Eugene Victor Debs* (New York: Russell & Russell, 1969), pp. 82–84.

4. Salvatore, pp. 115, 116.

5. Ginger, pp. 93–95, 100–101.

6. Salvatore, p. 121.

7. Ibid., pp. 118–123.

8. David R. Papke, *The Pullman Case: The Clash of Labor and Capital in Industrial America* (Lawrence: University Press of Kansas, 1999), pp. 17–19.

9. Papke, pp. 20–27.

10. Ginger, p. 123.

11. Ibid., pp. 121–128.

12. Papke, pp. 27–31.

13. Salvatore, pp. 132–137.

14. Papke, pp. 32–35.

15. Ibid., pp. 38–50.

16. Ibid., pp. 50–79.

17. Salvatore, pp. 138–146.

18. Ginger, pp. 172–181.

Chapter 5. From Democrat to Socialist

1. Ray Ginger, *The Bending Cross: A Biography of Eugene Victor Debs* (New York: Russell & Russell, 1969), pp. 182–188.

2. Ibid., pp. 71, 116, 151, 163.

3. Harold W. Currie, *Eugene V. Debs* (Boston: Twayne Publishers, 1976), pp. 32–34.

4. Nick Salvatore, *Eugene V. Debs: Citizen and Socialist* (Urbana: University of Illinois Press, 1982), p. 161.

5. Ginger, pp. 192–193.

6. Salvatore, pp. 161–162.

7. Currie, pp. 35–38.

8. Ginger, pp. 197–198.

9. Salvatore, pp. 162–167.

Chapter 6. Debs Runs for President

1. James Darsey, *The Prophetic Tradition and Radical Rhetoric in America* (New York: New York University Press, 1997), pp. 93–95, 200–204.

2. Ray Ginger, *The Bending Cross: A Biography of Eugene Victor Debs* (New York: Russell & Russell, 1969), p. 208.

3. Nick Salvatore, *Eugene V. Debs: Citizen and Socialist* (Urbana: University of Illinois Press, 1982), pp. 174–176.

4. Ibid., pp. 183–186.

5. Ginger, pp. 212–213.

6. Salvatore, pp. 188–190.

7. Ginger, pp. 213–221.

8. Ginger, p. 221.

9. Salvatore, pp. 206–210.

10. Ginger, p. 221.

11. Ibid., pp. 208, 230–233.

12. Salvatore, pp. 220–221.

13. Ibid., p. 221.

14. Ibid., pp. 221, 236–238.

15. Ginger, p. 279.

16. Ibid., pp. 279–283.

17. Ibid., p. 283.

18. Ibid.

19. Ibid., pp. 53–54, 286–289.

20. Salvatore, pp. 71–72, 140–141, 217–218.

21. Ginger, pp. 319–320.

22. Ibid., p. 320.

23. Salvatore, p. 213.

24. Ibid., p. 242.

25. Ibid.

26. Ibid., p. 264.

Chapter 7. Debs Goes to Prison

1. Harold W. Currie, *Eugene V. Debs* (Boston: Twayne Publishers, 1976), pp. 44–45.

2. Ray Ginger, *The Bending Cross: A Biography of Eugene Victor Debs* (New York: Russell & Russell, 1969), pp. 328–337.

3. Ginger, pp. 338–344.

4. Ibid., pp. 345–354.

5. Nick Salvatore, *Eugene V. Debs: Citizen and Socialist* (Urbana: University of Illinois Press, 1982), pp. 286–291.

6. Ginger, pp. 358–384.

7. Salvatore, pp. 308–312.

8. Ibid., pp. 313–325.

9. Eugene V. Debs, *Walls and Bars: Prisons and Prison Life in the "Land of the Free"* (Chicago: Charles H. Kerr, 2000), p. 164.

10. Salvatore, pp. 326–328.

11. Ibid., pp. 328–341.

Chapter 8. Debs: Failure or Success?

1. Nick Salvatore, *Eugene V. Debs: Citizen and Socialist* (Urbana: University of Illinois Press, 1982), pp. 155, 308–311, 328.

2. Ray Ginger, *The Bending Cross: A Biography of Eugene Victor Debs* (New York: Russell & Russell, 1969), pp. 458–459.

FURTHER READING

Colman, Penny. *Strike!: The Bitter Struggle of American Workers from Colonial Times to the Present.* Brookfield, Conn.: Millbrook Press, 1995.

Constantine, J. Robert, ed. *Gentle Rebel: Letters of Eugene V. Debs.* Champaign: University of Illinois Press, 1994.

Jarnow, Jesse. *Oil, Steel, and Railroads: America's Big Businesses in the Late 1800s.* New York: Rosen Publishing Group, Inc., 2003.

Laughlin, Rosemary. *The Pullman Strike of 1894: American Labor Comes of Age.* Greensboro, N.C.: Morgan Reynolds, Inc., 1999.

McKissack, Patricia and Frederick. *A Long Hard Journey: The Story of the Pullman Porter.* New York: Walker & Company, 1995

Meltzer, Milton. *Bread and Roses: The Struggle of American Labor, 1865–1915.* Bridgewater, N.J.: Replica Books, 1999.

Mofferd, Juliet H., ed. *Talkin' Union: The American Labor Movement.* Carlisle, Mass.: Discovery Enterprises, Ltd., 1997.

INTERNET ADDRESSES

Eugene V. Debs Internet Archive. n.d. <http://www.marxists.org/archive/debs>.

"The Eugene Victor Debs Collection." *Leonard H. Axe Library, Pittsburg State University.* © 2000. <http://library.pittstate.edu/spcoll/ndxevdebs.html>.

Official Site of the Eugene V. Debs Foundation. n.d. <http://www.eugenevdebs.com>.

INDEX